Principles
of
Metaphysics

Douglas P. McManaman

DPM Publishing
Aurora, Ontario

Registered with the Canadian Intellectual Property Office

DPM also publishes its books in a variety of electronic formats.

Library and Archives Canada Cataloguing in Publication

McManaman, Douglas
Principles of Metaphysics
Aurora, Ontario: DPM Publishing. 2016

ISBN: 978-0-9948233-2-8

Cover by Jennifer Johnson, 2016

Dedication

For Rado Krevs
Devoted teacher and thinker

Table of Contents

Author's Preface

This book was written only because a friend of mine, Matthew Schaeffer, who a day after receiving his PhD in Philosophy, asked me to write it; a small book on first principles, much like *A Preface to Metaphysics*, by Jacques Maritain, but one much simpler and easier to read. This book is hardly in the same league as Maritain's *Preface*, but I've never had any other goal in my writing than to provide a stepping stone to the works of the great thinkers. They have brought so much to my life and continue to do so, but most people can't read them; they lack the conceptual framework not to mention the time to make their way through their works. My primary desire is and has always been to provide steps that permit the layman to begin to enter through the thresholds of these great works.

Imagine trying to find a phone number for a specific person in a phone book that haphazardly contains the names and numbers of everyone in the city, that is, without the order the alphabet provides. It would take forever to find the number. A slightly better scenario is to imagine having to find a name and number in a phone book in which all the names are arranged according to the order of the alphabet—as the content of a phone book is so arranged—, but without a knowledge of the alphabet. The book is ordered, but one lacks a knowledge of the very principles of that order. Finding a number would also be quite an ordeal, but the obstacle can easily be overcome simply by learning the alphabet.

Of course, knowing how to readily find someone's phone number on the basis of alphabetic principles is one thing, knowing what is behind that name and number, that is, the rich details that characterize the life of the person whose number it is, is quite another. Metaphysics, it seems to me, is much like the former—knowing the principles, which do not, however, provide the richer details. The first principles of metaphysics enable us to find the right name and number, as it were, in a book that contains a vast amount of information, and in a reasonable amount of time, because reality is ordered. Without the fundamental principles of the philosophy of being, a person can find himself wasting a great deal of time pondering questions that cannot be answered by science, or hanging on to positions that might appear to follow from scientific premises, but in fact do no such thing.

The first principles of speculative reason are known intuitively and, initially at least, pre-consciously. They govern human reasoning on a very general level. But explicitly articulating those principles and drawing out some of their implications can go a long way in helping a person avoid a great deal of unnecessary confusion, in particular the confusion that results from failing to distinguish between different ways of knowing, i.e., science, mathematics, and philosophy, which are like the discontinuous layers of a cake. People are often unaware of the contradictions and inconsistencies in their thinking, and the root of such confusion, I believe, is in a lack of explicit understanding of the implications of those intuitively grasped principles. One ends up treating one layer as though it were the entire cake.

Metaphysics is the philosophy of being. The object is not being as living, or being as mobile, or being as human, etc., but being as being (insofar as it 'is'). The fundamental question is: "What does it mean to be?"

Now being is first; there is nothing prior to being. Before I know anything specific about a thing, at the very least I know that it 'is'. Being is fundamental; it is basic. Hence, metaphysics is first philosophy, and not epistemology or the theory of knowledge, and not physics. It is being that is given in knowledge; for when I know something, at the very least I know that 'something is'. And as a rule of thumb, I am aware of myself as subject only when knowing something other than myself, that is, when knowing something as object (of my knowledge); I do not know myself as subject except while knowing something as object—even when I make myself the object of thought, that knowledge is accompanied by a knowledge of myself as subject.

To understand some of the fundamental principles of being *as* being is to come away with a basic knowledge, a very general knowledge, a knowledge of something ultimate. By no means, however, is this knowledge complete and all-encompassing, at least not intensively. It is only all-encompassing extensively, that is, insofar as whatever is, is, and so a knowledge of the first principles of being is a knowledge of all things, at the most basic or fundamental level. But one can no more derive a precise knowledge of phenomena from a knowledge of the most general principles of metaphysics than a person can steer a motor vehicle, by remote control, through a crowded city on a winter day from on high sitting in a helicopter. To steer successfully, one needs to be familiar with the road conditions and able to read the various road signs, i.e., yield and stop signs, not to mention traffic lights and looking out for pedestrians, etc., all of which is outside the purview of someone high up in a helicopter. All he can do is provide a general direction—an important task, but far from providing a complete and sufficient knowledge of reality. Having said that, the view from a mountain top, although lacking in the rich detail that the ground level provides, is nevertheless very exhilarating and is often well worth the difficult climb.

My hope is that this book will provide the layman with a general direction, a fundamental conceptual framework that can make life a little easier, as knowing the alphabet makes finding a name and number in a phone book a little easier. Coming to a sufficient understanding of all that is behind a single name is difficult enough; it is simply impossible for every name in the book—there is simply not enough time to become familiar with the rich mystery that every individual person is. Similarly, we only know a tiny fraction of all that reality has to reveal. Intellectual abstraction, however, is able to achieve much more than we tend to think, just as the abstracted entities of the mathematician—i.e., integers, fractions, complex numbers, points, lines, surfaces, etc., divested of sensible matter—permit her to do so much more than would otherwise be possible, if number were forever locked up in sensible matter.

An old theology professor of mine, Jean-Claude Petite, warned us all at the end of a seminar course on Gadamer's *Truth and Method* to be very careful of metaphysical abstractions. I was not sure if his warning was two edged, but it should have been. A person can become so comfortable in the abstract regions of the philosophy of being that he becomes downright lazy— he confuses the all-embracing extension of being with an all-encompassing and intensive grasp of reality. There is always a trade off when rising to higher levels of abstraction; knowledge is had at the expense of a knowledge of the rich and inexhaustible content of concrete phenomena. For example, one cannot pronounce on matters of economics using the most general principles of morality; or, if one's head habitually resides in the highest regions of abstraction, one risks overlooking the subtleties of hermeneutics, that is, one is unaware of the various possible meanings of a text and the large space of uncertainty that accompanies historical investigation. In short, one may quickly become an absolutist, habitually attributing a far greater level of certainty to one's conclusions than is warranted.

But the refusal to rise up the degrees of abstraction is arbitrary; one imposes unnecessary limits on oneself. The absurdity of such a decision with respect to mathematics is immediately obvious; it is less obviously absurd but equally limiting in the area of metaphysics. Indeed, one should be careful not to attempt to establish scientific conclusions on the basis of metaphysical principles, but one ought to be equally careful not to draw metaphysical conclusions on the basis of scientific knowledge. The former is a danger for the lazy minded who fail to appreciate the logic of the scientific method; the latter is a danger for the scientist who is no longer satisfied with doing science and now wants to do metaphysics, but is too lazy and often too proud to commit to the long and disciplined study of the great minds of the history of philosophy.

1 A Simple Demonstration of the Dangers of Reductionism

"Being" or "is" is the simplest idea. The reason is that the idea of being is indivisible. To demonstrate this, consider that any quantity is divisible into parts, either logically (inside the mind) or really (outside the mind). When divided, any of the resulting parts is outside the other part (or is 'other than' another part). For example, divide a circle into 8 parts, with each part looking like a piece of pie; each piece of the pie is outside (or other than) the other piece. To divide being into parts would render one part outside another, but outside of being is non-being, which is nothing. Thus, the idea of being is always one and indivisible. Thus, the idea of being is not a quantity.

It follows that a quantity, such as a circle, a piece of secondary matter like wood or iron, or a number, etc., is not identical with being; the reason is that a quantity is divisible (either logically or really), while being is not. Thus, a real existing quantity (i.e., a piece of iron) is not identical with being; rather, in some way it possesses being (it exercises existence either inside the mind or outside the mind). As a quantity, it is divisible; as a being, however, it is indivisible.

The scientific method is, among other things, reductionistic—it seeks to understand a whole by understanding its parts. However, this reductionism is logical, not real. A being, such as a cat, would be destroyed if the scientist's reductionism were made real (i.e., if he were to separate each part and study it). Rather, he distinguishes a plurality of parts (logically), but he does not separate the being into a plurality of parts—unless it is already dead. Thus, we don't really divide being, that is, the being we are studying, we do so only logically (in the mind only). When we divide something logically, we don't destroy it really. But we do destroy our understanding of that being if, when dividing it logically, we forget that it is a unity, that is, a being. As being, it is indivisible; as quantified, it is divisible.

If being is indivisible, then being cannot be understood in terms of something other than it, or in terms of something outside of it; for there is nothing outside of being. Thus, being cannot be understood in terms of measurement, because to measure something is to understand it *in terms other than the terms one is measuring.* A quantified being, for example, can be measured, but what is understood through measurement is the quantity of the thing that is measured, the terms of which are to be found in the measure (i.e., centimeters on a ruler). In other words, the thing or being is understood in terms of quantity, not on its own terms, that is, not in terms of being (being is not identical to quantity).

Finally, if there is no simplest idea, then there is no first idea, which would mean that every idea can be broken down into a simpler idea still. But if understanding a complex idea depends on understanding its simpler constituents, then it is impossible that there be no first and simplest idea; for one would not know anything definitively. The reason is one's knowledge would depend on knowing an indefinite number of factors; thus, one's knowledge would remain forever indefinite. Hence, it is not true that "if one cannot measure something, that something is unknowable". Nor is it true that a single being is nothing other than the sum of its parts; if it were simply a multiplicity of parts, it would not be a "being" as such.

2 The Principle of Contradiction

The idea of being, which is the simplest idea, arises ultimately from our contact with real being—as all our ideas ultimately arise from the realm of the real. We live in a world of beings or things. It is being that is given in knowledge; for what I know first and foremost, and at the very least, is that "something is". The reason I say this is that nothing else can be given first, because being is first; there is nothing prior to being. If something is prior to being, then whatever it is, it either 'is' or 'is not'. If it 'is', then being is still first; if it 'is not', then it is nothing, and then it would follow that nothing is prior to being. Either way, being is absolutely first.

We can test this claim by reflecting upon our own knowing. Given that something is an object of knowledge for me, I may not know precisely 'what' it is; I may not even know 'generally' what it is (i.e., whether it is a substance or a property of a substance, or even an illusion); at the very least, however, I know that it is— either logically (in the mind) or really (outside the mind).

Any being we apprehend—either in the world or in the mind (i.e., the idea of the number five)—necessarily is *as long as it is*. I qualify this with 'as long as it is', because we are not aware of any being in our direct and immediate experience that *cannot not exist* (i.e., is eternal and absolutely necessary). But a being (such as the cat, the plant, or a carbon atom, etc.,) indeed necessarily exists *as long as it exists*. The cat I now see outside my window exists, and so the claim I make at this moment that "The cat outside does not exist" is necessarily false, as opposed to "possibly false".

In other words, nothing can both be and not be at the same time and in the same respect. This is the principle of contradiction. The logical formulation of this principle is that *nothing can be both true and not true at the same time and in the same respect.* So the proposition that there is no cat outside my window is necessarily not true as long as there really is a cat outside my window. Thus, what is true follows upon what is (being). In other words, not only is "one" a property of being (whatever is, is one insofar as it is), "true" is also a property of being (whatever is, is true insofar as it is).

So although truth might be difficult to acquire in many areas of study, such as the truth of a person's guilt, or the truth of what actually happened two or three centuries ago, or the truth of string theory or whether or not raising the minimum wage will truly raise a nation's standard of living, etc., it is simply not possible that "there is no truth". The claim violates the principle of contradiction, for it proposes that it is true that there is no truth, as do other self-refuting claims, such as "possessing certainty is not possible on any level", or "I know that knowledge is impossible", etc.

Reductionism can also be looked upon from the angle of the principle of contradiction. Being is indivisible, as was said earlier. Whatever is, is one insofar as it is. Reductionism regards the whole as merely the sum of its parts—either methodologically (as one does when doing science) or philosophically (as in scientism).[1] But nothing can be a multiplicity and a unity at the same time and in the same respect, but only in different respects. Hence, a single being is not a multiplicity, otherwise it is not a single being, but beings. The multiplicity of parts, rather, belong to the whole; for they are 'parts of the whole'.

Schrodinger's Cat

But doesn't Schrodinger's thought experiment, Schrodinger's Cat, refute the principle of contradiction? It does not, because it is simply impossible to deny the principle of contradiction without using it, that is, without affirming it. To deny any principle or proposition is to claim that its affirmation is false; and to claim that it is false is to propose that anyone who affirms it is mistaken (is wrong), or has been proven wrong (i.e., by Schrodinger).

Schrodinger's thought experiment is simply a demonstration of the apparent conflict between what quantum theory reveals about the nature of matter on the subatomic level and what we observe to be true about matter on the macroscopic level. That there is an apparent conflict or a kind of quantum weirdness is true, which is why Schrodinger came up with the thought experiment. To deny it by claiming that there is no difference between the nature of matter on both levels is to make a false claim.

And so already, up to this point, the principle of contradiction remains true; for to deny the principle of contradiction would permit the denial of any kind of quantum weirdness. Furthermore, that hydrocyanic acid is a radioactive substance is true; to assert that the substance is not radioactive is false. Both cannot be true and not true at one and the same time and in the same respect. Finally, let us assume that something exists in a superposition of states. Again, to make that claim implies that the principle of contradiction is true. The reason is that if one were to say that nothing exists in a superposition of states, that claim would be false—if there is indeed such a thing as a superposition of states. In other words, we can think of "particles" as existing across all the possible states at the same time, although we may not be able to visualize such a thing.

To assert definitively that such a superposition of states is impossible, or to simply deny Heisenberg's uncertainty principle, is to make a false assertion—if a superposition of states is possible and the Heisenberg uncertainty principle is true. In order to make definite claims about the quantum level of reality, the principle of contradiction must be true. Finally, let it be a given that an observation affects an outcome; if that is true, then an observation definitely affects an outcome and denying this would be false. If, however, the principle of contradiction is false, then it is, in the same respect and simultaneously, true, and denying it would be pointless. In fact, denying anything would ultimately be pointless, because to deny something would be to affirm it, and to affirm it would be to deny it, which is of course entirely absurd and not permitted by the very principle one is denying, and the very principle one is using to deny it. And so if someone interprets scientific data in a way that results in the denial of a self-evident first principle, we can be assured that the interpretation is flawed.

3 The Principle of Identity

The principle of identity is simply a different formulation of the principle of contradiction; it runs: *each being is what it is*. In other words, a carrot is a carrot, not a hippopotamus. It is not possible to prove through a demonstrative syllogism that the principle of identity is necessarily true, because in order to prove anything at all, one depends on the principle. For example, we conclude that it is necessarily true that John is rational because "All men are rational" and "John is a man". Those two premises, however, depend on the principle of identity: *each being is what it is*. In other words, we are talking about "man" and "rational", not fruit trees and sweetness.

Does that mean we do not really "know" whether or not the principle of identity is true and that it is merely an assumption? Only if we identify knowledge exclusively with a reasoned conclusion. But if we identify knowledge exclusively with a reasoned conclusion, then ultimately the truth of our conclusions is founded on an assumption or set of assumptions. This would imply that, ultimately, certain knowledge is not possible; the entire body of science would be little more than a large edifice built on an assumption or set of assumptions.

But knowledge is not limited to the reasoned conclusions of an argument from premises; rather, the *intuition* of the first principles counts as genuine knowledge, either conscious or preconscious. Being is given in knowledge, and everyone who knows anything at all knows first and foremost, immediately and intuitively, that 'is' is not identical with 'is not': being is not nothing, but something. If being is not identical to non-being, a being is identical to itself, that is, *each being is what it is*, not what it is not.

Seeing as we made brief remarks on reductionism in the previous two chapters, consider the following thought on reductionism in the light of the principle of identity. The classical reductionist regards the whole (i.e., the whole organism) as nothing other than the sum of its parts. But the parts of the whole, such as the organs, are nothing other than the sum of their constituent parts (i.e., cells); and these parts are nothing other than the sum of their own constituents parts, and so on. In other words, each thing is 'nothing other than…', which in turn is 'nothing other than…'. In short, nothing is what it is, but is *other than* what it is. Reductionism is thus inconsistent with the fundamental intuition of being and the basic law of identity.

Essence and Existence

But there is more packed into this principle that can be unraveled. A being is 'what' it 'is'. In other words, beings have a specific determination, a 'whatness'. A carrot, a cat, a watermelon and a rose bush are determinate beings or things, not indeterminate; that is, they are intelligible (the intellect can determine what they are, at least generally if not precisely). We may not know exactly "what" something is, but we naturally desire to know "what" it is, which is why we are inclined to ask a most fundamental question: "What is it?"

We don't immediately know what a thing is completely when we apprehend the very existence of that being, which is why we wish to know what it is more fully. In other words, we don't know beings from within (as we do ourselves), but from without, which is why we observe them in their activity. It is through the activity of a being that we come to know "what" it is more specifically; for it is activity that discloses or unveils the specific determination of that being.

This suggests that knowing "what" something is and knowing "that" something is are two distinct intellectual apprehensions. I know that something is, for example, I know that there is something moving around in my backyard garden, but I don't quite know what it is. After a while, I make the inference that it is an animal of some kind, because it seems to be moving on its own—however, I am not entirely certain that it is an animal. Suddenly, an animal dashes out and scurries under the fence; but I have never seen such a creature before; I am not familiar with such an animal. It returns later on and so I begin to observe its behavior, hoping to come to a richer understanding of 'what it is'. If I have a good mind for science, I might even create the conditions for a controlled experience (experiment) and study it in greater detail, that is, with greater precision. Gradually, my knowledge of 'what' it is increases; but my apprehension of its existence (i.e., 'that' it is) is not subject to increase. Being is not divisible into parts outside of parts; it is not a quantity, thus it is not subject to more or less: *it either is or is not, there is no in between* (the principle of the excluded middle).

It follows that *what a thing is essentially* is distinct from its *existence*. A cat, for example, *has* existence (has being, or exercises existence), but *it is* feline—we would not say that a cat is existence. What it 'has' and what it 'is' are not identical. My knowledge of 'what it is' is subject to increase, my knowledge 'that it is' is not subject to increase.

Moreover, we began by focusing on the idea of being, but the idea of being ultimately has its roots in the apprehension of real being (outside the mind). The idea of being as it exists inside the mind is maximally general; as such, it does not have a great deal of content. However, outside the mind, being is the richest in intelligible content; for without the very act of existing, there is nothing to know. For example, I can come to know what a cat is to an extent that is very precise and full of detail, but knowing 'what it is' does not tell me whether or not 'it is'—I have no idea whether there are any more cats left in the world—they could have become extinct for all I know. Their extinction, moreover, does not alter my knowledge of what they are essentially.

But my apprehension of a real existing cat involves an apprehension of something more than "what it is"— I apprehend something more than its essence (i.e., what it is essentially); I apprehend its existence. The intelligible content of its existence is distinct from and over and above the intelligible content of its essence— even though both apprehensions are simultaneous. Without the act of existing, which I apprehend in knowing it, the cat is nothing at all.

It is by virtue of this distinction between what a thing is and its very *act of existing* that I was forced earlier to add the qualification "as long as it is" when addressing 'necessity': the cat outside my window necessarily exists as long as exists. In other words, it need not exist. For example, 50 years ago that cat did not exist, and 50 years from now, it will not exist. Hence, its existence is not necessary, but contingent. This means that it is a possible being that at this time actually exists, or possesses an act of existing. And although it exists now, it is possible for it not to exist. Thus, it is not a necessary being, but a contingent being, and its existence is only necessary as long as it is.

4 The Necessary Being

In chapter two, it was said that we are not aware of any being in our direct and immediate experience that cannot not exist (i.e., is eternal and necessary). If something exists necessarily, it cannot not exist. But a being (such as the cat, the plant, or a carbon atom, etc.,) necessarily exists *as long as it exists*, which suggests that it can indeed cease to be.

Let us ask the question then: "Does a necessary being exist?" And is there any way to show that a necessary being exists? Moreover, what does it mean to be a necessary being?

Firstly, a necessary being is a being that cannot not exist, but exists necessarily. If it exists necessarily, then it always existed (i.e., is eternal). If it is eternal, it was not created. This, in part at least, is what most people mean by "God". So, does God exist?

I will argue here that the existence of God (the necessary Being) can be demonstrated rather easily and concisely. To do so, allow me to quote Gottfried Wilhelm Leibniz, one of the inventors of Calculus, who formulated the following concise argument: "If the necessary Being is possible, it exists".[2]

Of course, one will inevitably ask: "Why?" The answer is: because it is the necessary Being, and a necessary being cannot not exist. Therefore, it exists, unless of course it is impossible that a necessary being exists. It would be impossible for the necessary Being to exist if 'necessity' and 'being' were mutually exclusive in the sense that they cannot exist in one and the same subject, as 'square' and 'circle' cannot exist in one and the same subject (it is impossible that there exists a square circle). But 'necessity' and 'being' are not mutually exclusive in terms of existing in one and the same subject; in fact, every contingent being (non-necessary being, i.e., you, me, the cat, the oak tree, a blade of grass, etc.) is necessary as long as it exists. Existence gives rise to necessity.

What makes this proof difficult for some to grasp is the fact that it is impossible to prove the existence of a contingent being through the idea of that being, because the 'idea' of a contingent being (its essence) is a possibility for being. In other words, knowing everything about 'feline' or 'canine' (what they are) does not tell you whether or not they actually are (actually exist); it is possible for cats to exist, but to know whether or not they do requires that we directly apprehend their existence. One cannot leap from the idea of a thing (its essence) to the existence of the thing.

The only exception to this rule, however, is the necessary Being (at least according to Leibniz and those who regard his argument as sound, as does this author). Why? Because the necessary Being is not a possible being like everything else, but a necessary Being, a Being that cannot not exist, but exists necessarily. If it is logically possible, then it exists. Thus, God exists.

A possible objection to this argument is that one can insert "being" into the definition of anything, thereby rendering it necessary, i.e., an exotic fruit, a unicorn, a Hobbit, etc. In other words, theists indeed have a concept of God, but "being" is simply inserted into that concept, making being a part of it, and the conclusion is then drawn that God necessarily exists. Moreover, the claim is often made that it is a circular argument, an instance of the fallacy of begging the question (assuming the point that needs to be proven).

The objection, however, fails because inserting "being" into a concept essentially reduces it to the necessary Being. In other words, making being a part of a concept, such as an exotic or an imaginary fruit, utterly transforms the concept into something else entirely, namely, the necessary Being, of which there can only be one, as will be shown.

Consider that whatever belongs to the concept of a thing belongs to it necessarily. "Rational" belongs necessarily to the concept of man, and "three-sided" belongs necessarily to the concept of triangle, etc. Inserting "being" into a concept indeed renders it necessary, but what is left of everything else in the definition? Nothing is left, except being.

Take the concept of "dinosaur"; it includes a number of parts, such as "living", "sentient", "cold-blooded", and "vertebrate", etc. These parts of the concept are not parts of one another. For example, "vertebrate" is not part of the concept "living"; for if it were, all living things would be vertebrates—and anything that is not a vertebrate would not be living, which of course is false. In the same way, "sentient" is not part of the concept "living"; for if it were, all living things would be sentient; yet flowers are living but not sentient, etc. "Sentient" is outside the concept "living", as are "vertebrate" and "cold-blooded".

In other words, each part of the concept is "outside of" every other part; they are "parts outside of parts". But insert "being" as a part of the concept and something happens: all the other parts (sentient, cold-blooded, vertebrate, etc.) are now outside of "being", since all parts are outside of one another. Outside of being, however, is non-being, and non-being is nothing. Thus, nothing is outside of the "part" being, which means that being is not a part, but the whole.

The entire concept is reduced to "being itself", and whatever belongs to the concept belongs to it necessarily. Therefore, being itself is alone necessary. Inserting "being" into a concept, such as "dinosaur" does not give us a dinosaur that necessarily exists; rather, it reduces it from "dinosaur" to the necessary Being (God).

Finally, if being or existence were part of "vertebrate", "living", "sentient", "cold-blooded", "fruit", "man", etc., then these latter would necessarily exist and could not not exist, which is manifestly false. And so being or existence is not part of the concept of anything, but is rather the whole of the necessary Being.

There can only be one necessary Being for the same reason that being cannot be one part alongside other parts; for if there were two necessary Beings, what would distinguish this necessary Being from that necessary Being? It would have to be something that they are not or do not share in common. What are they in common? They are Being. And since outside of being is non-being, nothing distinguishes them, and so the necessary Being is ultimately one, not many.

A contingent being whose concept does not include being or existence can only be known to exist empirically, and not logically, that is, not by a consideration of the concept alone. The necessary Being, on the other hand, cannot be known empirically (through sensation), but it can be known to exist by a consideration of the concept alone (logically, or *a priori*). Nothing, in fact, is easier to prove than God's existence, which is really the answer to atheist Bertrand Russell's question that he said he would put to God were he to stand before Him one day: "Sir, why did you take such pains to hide yourself?"

5 The Principle of Sufficient Reason

We know immediately and intuitively that 'is' is not identical to 'is not'. Thus, we know intuitively that from nothing comes nothing. In other words, 'nothing' cannot be an antecedent that explains a consequent. In other words, one cannot claim the reason that explains w is not x, y, or z, or even w itself, but no reason at all;[3] such an explanation is no explanation, which would mean that the consequent is in principle incapable of being understood (or explained), not merely by us, but absolutely. We could not even call it a consequent. It would be both intelligible (insofar as being is intelligible), but it would have no sufficient reason for being (either within itself or outside itself), thus no ground either in itself or outside itself that accounts for it. In that sense, it would be a pure enigma, or intelligible and unintelligible at the same time and in the same respect. We'd be inclined to try to understand it, but no sufficient reason could be discovered, in principle, that would satisfy the intellect. It is not that we have never encountered such a thing; rather, it is impossible for there to be such a thing. Being is intelligible, and as nothing can both be and not be at the same time and in the same respect, nothing can be both intelligible and unintelligible at the same time and in the same respect—only in different respects, i.e., unintelligible to us, but intelligible in principle.

We are thus led to another first principle, namely, the principle of sufficient reason: *Everything which is, to the extent to which it is, possesses a sufficient reason for its being so that it is capable of explaining itself to the intellect*. In other words, *whatever is, has that whereby it is, either in itself or in another.*[4] The very word 'sufficient' is from the Latin, *sufficere*, which means to ground, to lay a foundation under, or to supply as a substitute, one that is adequate. It means to make "up to", a foundation that is adequate to what it is expected to support.

The antecedent, or reason by virtue of which something is, cannot be less than the consequent, but equal to or greater than it, just as the capacity of a foundation (i.e., a capacity to hold 200 pounds) cannot be less than the weight it supports (i.e., 400 pounds). Such a foundation would be inadequate, for it would collapse. In other words, the reason that explains the consequent must be sufficient; otherwise the intellect remains insufficiently satisfied. It remains unsatisfied because we know intuitively that from nothing comes nothing, and so if the effect is greater than the "reason for" it, or the cause of it, to that extent it (the consequent) remains unexplained or unaccounted for. If it rained only 3 inches last night, but there is 12 inches of water in the rain gauge, then the rainfall is insufficient to explain entirely the 12 inches in the rain gauge; it explains 3 inches, but the remaining 9 inches remains unaccounted for.

The principle of identity, which we discussed in the previous chapter, is that "each being is what it is". A rational animal is just that, an animal that can act in a way that is explained by an appeal to her capacity for rational activity (her rational nature). Another possible formulation of the principle of identity is *whatever is, is determined*. If it is not determined, then it is unintelligible. The reason is that indeterminacy pure and simple is unintelligible; in other words, "what it is" cannot be determined, because it completely lacks determination. In other words, it lacks 'limits' (terminals) that would enable us to distinguish it from anything else. Thus, to the extent that something is, it is determined; to the extent that it is 'not', it is undetermined.

Pure potentiality is pure indeterminacy; as such, it is not actually anything. Indeterminacy pure and simple would lack all unity or oneness; for whatever 'is' is one and indivisible insofar as it is. Pure indeterminacy or pure potentiality is thus unintelligible, since it lacks unity and being.

Pure potentiality, however, is not the same as nothing, even though it is not actually anything. The idea of potentiality has reference to actuality, while 'nothing' does not (nothing has no reference). It is in this aspect of 'reference to' that potentiality or indeterminacy is intelligible. Pure indeterminacy lacks all determination, therefore it lacks the determination of unity or oneness; thus, pure indeterminacy is pure plurality without oneness, which of course is itself unintelligible; for it is unity that renders a multiplicity intelligible (how can a plurality of currency, for example, be understood except in reference to a unit of currency, such as the euro or the dollar?).

Consider two pure potentialities or two pure indeterminacies (which is impossible, strictly speaking, because 'two' implies a unit of some kind, which is a kind of determination): one potentiality cannot be distinguished from another potentiality; for there is no 'termination' or limit that can distinguish the two; moreover, pure potentiality lacks any and all actuality or content on the basis of which one could make a distinction.

A number of points follow from the above. To understand indeterminacy (or potentiality) is impossible on its own terms, but it is intelligible only in terms of or in reference to some sort of actuality. It would have to exist in composition with an actuality of some kind, for example, an actual piece of white paper that is potentially written on, or an organism that has the potentiality to grow, such as a plant. That actuality is a determinate something. Other examples include a human being that has a potentiality to learn calculus, a cat that has the potentiality to see in the dark, and a plant has the potentiality to grow, an oxygen atom that has the potentiality to react with another substance, etc.

A plant, however, does not have the potentiality to see, nor does a cat have the potentiality to learn calculus; and there is no reason to infer that a cat has the potentiality to learn calculus, for it is not evident in its activity. We would be astounded if a cat were to pose a question about calculus or history, but we are not surprised when a human being asks such questions, unless the question is exceptionally brilliant. The reason for our lack of surprise is that there is sufficient reason to explain the origin of the question. The antecedent is something, a determinate kind of thing, namely an existing rational nature; for a person with a rational nature seeks to understand the reasons for things and the intelligible relationships between things that exist either outside the mind or inside the mind (such as numbers or other abstracted quantities). The potentialities of a cat are limited to sense perception and the appetites that follow upon it; so there is nothing unusual about a cat that sees a mouse and pursues it.

In other words, a thing cannot give what it does not have (from nothing comes nothing); a cat does not possess a rational nature, so it cannot give evidence of a rational nature; it cannot perform rational acts, because each being is limited (determined) to what it is; it is not open to being *what it is not* without ceasing to be what it is (in other words, it is open to being something else entirely, but only at the expense of ceasing to be what it is; i.e., a living organism is potentially a corpse).

Activity does not arise out of pure potentiality or pure indeterminacy, and the reason is that the effect cannot be greater than the cause, and actuality is greater than potentiality; for pure potentiality is not actually anything. Strictly speaking, to have a potentiality to something is to lack that something. Hence, activity arises out of an actuality, an actual existing nature that has potentialities to further acts or activity. This is true even if we do not know specifically what that actuality is. To suggest that act arises out of potentiality pure and simple is to suggest that something does impart what it does not have, which is contradictory. Activity arises out of an actuality that possesses some sort of potentiality to activity.

We said above that potentiality or indeterminacy is unintelligible as such; hence, a being is unintelligible to the degree it has potentiality that is non-actualized (or unrealized). That is precisely why we are inclined to study how something behaves or reacts with other substances; we wish to understand it more fully. Before it acts, we are in the dark, to some degree at least, as to what it is. In acting, a being reveals its specific determination or nature. Prior to that unveiling, it is intelligible to the degree that it is actual, but it is unintelligible to the degree that it is potential (or indeterminate). Activity is the actualization of a potentiality; thus, activity unveils the specific nature of a thing (what it is and what it can do).

And so denying the principle of sufficient reason is

as irrational as denying the principle of contradiction. The principle of sufficient reason is the driving force behind the quest for understanding; without the first principles, including sufficient reason, science is simply impossible. The scientific quest is precisely a quest for the sufficient reason for things.

6 Every Change Presupposes a Subject

Being is intelligible, and there is a twofold intelligibility to being: the intelligibility of the "what" (what a thing is essentially) and the intelligibility of the act of existing (the 'is'). A being is a composite of the two. The apprehension of the former is subject to increasing depths and precision, the apprehension of the latter is not subject to increase: for a being either is or is not, there is no in between.

Potentiality or indeterminacy is not a principle of intelligibility, but is actually a source of unintelligibility; a being is unintelligible to the degree that it is in potentiality. Change is precisely the realization (or actualization) of a being's potentiality, insofar as it is in potentiality. If act is the principle of intelligibility, a being is unintelligible to the degree that it lacks that actualization. I cannot know a student's mark for a test that has not yet been written, I do not know what a carpenter has in mind to make by simply looking at the planks of wood he intends to use and which are only potentially that which he has in mind to make; I do not know whether a thing that is perfectly immobile is alive or not. If it is alive, it can move itself, and it is only when it actually moves itself that I can be assured that it is indeed alive (activity unveils 'what' a thing is).

But only an actual being can change, because potentiality is only intelligible in reference to an actuality (pure potentiality is purely unintelligible and is not actually anything). It is being that renders change intelligible; thus, *pure becoming is unintelligible.*[5] It would have no subject, and thus no identifiable terminal. In other words, a change is only meaningful to the degree that it possesses a direction (consider the French word for meaning: *sens*, which is also 'direction').

The two terminals that render a change determinate are *that from which* the change proceeds and *that to which* the change proceeds. A simple example is an apple that changes from a green apple to a red apple. The two terminals are green and red. But without a subject that undergoes the change, i.e., the apple, it remains entirely unintelligible. It is *something* that changes. It is a green apple that is undergoing change, or an artifact that is moving from north to south, etc. Without that enduring subject, change is unintelligible; thus, pure becoming is indeterminate (without terminals) and thus unintelligible.

And so every change presupposes a subject that undergoes the change, which is the actualization of a being's potentiality, either to become red, or to become larger, or sweeter, or disposed in a certain way, etc. Pure becoming is as unintelligible as a world without the principle of identity; a world of pure becoming is a world in which each being is not what it is. It is only being that becomes, not becoming that becomes.

We also have the luxury of knowing this from within, through self-knowledge. In knowing anything, I know myself as *the subject that knows an object*. In fact, I only become aware of myself *as subject* when knowing something *as the object of* my thought; and even when I make myself the object of my own thought, I am at the same time aware of myself as subject of that act of knowing. It is I who have undergone all these changes, whether they be intellectual changes, or physical changes, emotional changes, etc.

7 The Principle of Finality

On the basis of the principle that every change presupposes a subject, we can articulate another first principle, namely, the principle of finality: *every agent acts for an end.* The end is that for the sake of which there is coming-to-be (change). Without an end, there is no terminal to which the agent tends, and to that degree, the change remains unintelligible. A vehicle that is moving indefinitely is not going anywhere; its movement is intelligible to the degree that it began at some point, and it is intelligible insofar as it continues to reach points along a trajectory, but it is unintelligible insofar as it has no end to which it moves. We are naturally inclined to inquire of someone: "Where are you going?" The reason is that we wish to make sense out of that motion, but if the agent is not going anywhere, then ultimately we cannot make sense out of its movement. But we study the motions of things precisely in order to determine the end to which it moves, believing all the while that the indeterminacy is merely in us, that is, in our lack of understanding.

All agents act for an end, and it is the agent's activity that unveils just "what" the agent is. If the agent's activity unveils "what" it is, then the action is determinate and thus intelligible, for every agent is a determinate something, that is, a being of a particular nature, an intelligibly determinate entity. If the activity did not disclose, at least to some extent, the nature of the thing in question, then it would be pointless to observe things in their activity, and we'd never know "what" things are. Water is an essentially different kind of substance than oxygen; it acts differently. Oxygen, for example, does not put out fires, but water does put out fires. A human being completely surrounded by water would drown, but a human being surrounded by oxygen would live. If agents such as inanimate substances did not act for determinate ends, we would not know what to do with them, how they can be used for more remote purposes, such as putting out fires, or helping someone stay alive, or adding flavor to our food, cleaning ourselves, etc.

Thoughts on Chance

Without that end or terminal, the motion of a moving thing remains unintelligible (for it is act that renders things intelligible, but potentiality or indeterminacy is the principle of unintelligibility). A series of acts ordered to an end (i.e., putting on one's shoes, grabbing one's keys, opening and closing the door, locking the door, walking to the car and opening the car door, etc.) become ultimately intelligible by virtue of the end intended (she is going to her doctor's appointment). It is the end that "makes sense" out of (gives direction to) the movement.

It is not by chance that she put on her shoes, nor was it by chance that she took a left hand turn on Yonge Street in the direction of the doctor's office. But it was by chance that an old friend she hadn't seen in years was crossing the intersection at the precise moment she was stopped at the red light. That old friend was heading in another direction, and the act of walking across the intersection at that time was part of the series of acts ordered to a determinate end, namely, her intention to purchase groceries for the week. Both wonder: "What are the chances that we would meet after so long a separation at this very intersection in this city?"

Chance is an intersection of at least two independent series of acts ordered to an end. The intersection of the two long lost friends was a chance occurrence, which is only intelligible against the background of an occurrence or set of occurrences that are not chance happenings (i.e., going to the doctor and going to the grocery store). A disorder can only be understood in relation to what is ordered; an unintended happening can only be understood against the backdrop of what is intended.

Chance happenings occur all the time. When we pay attention to them, they can seem to be more frequent than non-chance occurrences—of course, they have to be less frequent, at least by a 2:1 ratio—, but we typically pay little attention to them because they are, as chance happenings, unintelligible. They have no intrinsic meaning. They are disorders, relatively speaking. We pay attention to acts that are intrinsically meaningful, that is, we pay attention to where we are going, and those actions are meaningful to us because they have a definite end—even if we are simply going out for a walk without a pre-determined route. All meaningful acts of ours, however, are surrounded by clouds of ambiguity, namely, the opacity and obscurity of chance occurrences.

That is why it is impossible for everything to be a matter of chance. If it were, we would not know it, because chance happenings are only understood to be what they are relative to ordered series of acts, that is, happenings that are not chance.

Thoughts on Randomness

It is not entirely absurd, however, to argue that everything happens according to laws of probability—whether it is true or what that means exactly is another matter altogether, something we should revisit. But chance and randomness are terms frequently used interchangeably, as if they mean the same thing. I prefer to distinguish them on the grounds that randomness—at least a certain kind of randomness—can be studied; it is intelligible. There is an order to events that are random, at least at some level—and as long as we are talking about a certain kind of randomness; but there is no order to events that are chance.

For example, one can take a needle and a piece of paper with lines separated by a distance that is the length of the needle. If one drops the needle onto the paper, the needle will at times land in between the lines, while at other times it will cut the line. The number of times it will cut the line is approximately $2/\pi$ or 64%. Have 250 people flip a fair coin 20 times and record how many times each one flips heads. Plot the result and we see the gradual emergence of a normal distribution, with approximately 68% flipping between 7-13 heads (one standard deviation from the mean). Such experiments, however, whether we use needles and carefully spaced lines, or carefully crafted dice or unbiased coins, presuppose order. They are ordered experiments consisting of acts ordered to an end, using artifacts that have a definite intelligible configuration, such as a pack of cards with exactly 13 diamonds, 13 clubs, 13 spades, and 13 hearts, or fair coins and unbiased dice. The entire result is an order that can be unveiled mathematically; and if the whole (the entire result) is nothing other than the sum of its parts (each coin toss or each drop of the needle) and the whole is ordered, then every part is ordered as well. In other words, ordered parts behave in a way that is orderly.

There is nothing surprising here, because activity unveils a prior order. It just happens that the parts that make up the whole (i.e., a coin flip or toss of a needle) are ordered in a way that we simply do not understand at this point. But this is not quite the same as what we typically mean by chance occurrences. A carefully configured experiment designed to measure randomness is potentially disturbed by a chance occurrence, such as an earthquake, or a dog that escapes from his leash and runs through the room and over the table on which you were conducting your experiment, or a bird that flies in and grabs a coin from the table, etc. These are chance occurrences that interfere with the probability calculus—one has to begin the experiment again. That an important personage misdialed and ended up calling me was not a random event, but a chance happening.

Whether chance is, on another level, something ordered and thus intelligible is something to consider, along with the question of what it means to say that the physical universe is governed by randomness. We do not, however, have enough behind us to do justice to these questions at this point.

8 The Principle of Causality: Thoughts on Relativity

It was said above that disorder can only be understood in relation to (or relative to) that which is ordered, and potentiality can only be understood in relation to what is actual. As well, left and right can only be understood in relation to the observer, and whether or not someone is tall can only be understood in relation to those in his or her immediate vicinity, or in relation to the overall average height of the community or country. And so the question naturally arises: "Is everything relative?"

This is not a difficult question to answer. We do so by assuming a position (such as 'everything is relative') and drawing out the logical implications in order to see whether it leads to absurdities. To understand a claim that is truly relative depends on certain conditions. First, we must know the subject of the relation, i.e., Janet, as in the proposition "Janet is tall". It is also necessary to know the ground or cause of the relation, which in this case is height. But the height of the subject is to be related to a term, just as a moving thing proceeds in the direction of a term or terminal. The term of the relation is, in this case, the average height of the people in the immediate vicinity, or the national average, etc. Without the term, such as the average height of the community, the relative proposition remains unintelligible (i.e., there is no absolute tall, nor absolute left side of a rock; the "left side" is only understood in relation to a term, i.e., it is the side that is to my left). This is similar to a motion that remains unintelligible to the degree that the terminal to which it tends is unknown.

Now, the claim is that everything is relative, but my understanding of the claim depends on understanding the term of the relation (i.e., those in her immediate vicinity, let's call this t_1). But that too is relative, which means understanding t_1 depends on my understanding of another term (t_2), and since this term is relative (since everything is relative), my understanding of t_2 depends on t_3, which in turn depends on my understanding of t_4, which in turn depends on...t_∞. If everything is relative, then my understanding of a relative claim depends on my understanding of an indefinite or infinite number of terms. The result is that I never achieve a definitive understanding of a relative claim. The reason is that possessing a definitive understanding of a relative proposition would depend on understanding an indefinite number of terms. This would mean my understanding would be forever indefinite or indeterminate, which in the end is no understanding at all. To possess a determinate understanding which is at the same time and in the same respect an indeterminate understanding is contradictory.

Hence, not everything is relative. There must be something that is understood not in relation to something else, but *in itself*. And of course, being is not understood in relation to anything outside of it, because outside of being is non-being, which is nothing. Neither is being understood in relation to its constituent parts, because being *as such* (not as quantity) has no constituent parts—being is not a quantity (rather, quantity is one mode of being alongside others). So being is intelligible in and of itself. I see that Janet is tall in relation to every other child in the gymnasium, but my apprehension of what Janet is (at least on a very general level) and her very act of existing are immediate (Janet is something, she is a being of some kind, and she is something that 'is').

Now a cause is a principle from which something proceeds with dependence. According to this definition, the genus is 'principle' (that from which something proceeds), and the specific difference is 'with dependence'. This means that my understanding of anything that is genuinely relative is "caused", insofar as it depends on a principle; for example, my understanding of the claim "Janet is tall" depends on my understanding of the ground of the relation, and the subject, but also the term of the relation (i.e., the heights of those in Janet's immediate vicinity, or the national average).

The principle of causality is grounded ultimately in the principle of contradiction: from nothing comes nothing ('is' is not identical to 'is not'). When we hear a knock at the door, we don't believe someone or something made that sound, nor do we conjecture; rather, we know someone or something made that sound (we might conjecture about who it was that made the sound, but not that there was a cause of the sound). We know immediately and intuitively that nothing moves itself from potentiality to actuality except by something already in actuality, which is a principle that is ultimately rooted in the principle of contradiction.

Potentiality and actuality are not identical; the latter is *more than* the former. And so we proceed to answer the door, not as a result of an inductive inference or probability judgment or through the force of habit, but rather because we know something, we are certain of something, namely, that the knock was caused by something other than the door.

Necessity arises from our apprehension of being—whatever is, necessarily is as long as it is. Moreover, 'is' is not identical to 'non-being' or 'nothing'; in other words, 'is' is not nothing, but something. To change is to acquire 'being' at some level. A being that was in potentiality to a perfection[6] of some kind, that is, to an 'is' of some kind, acquires that 'is' (whether we are talking about a new quality, or quantity, or relation, or place, or posture, etc.). 'Is' does not arise from 'nothing', but from something, and the necessity of that apprehension is grounded in our apprehension of being. And so although I do not perceive a knocker, nor perceive with my senses the very idea of necessity, I have a knowledge which carries the force of necessity that someone or something caused that sound, I just don't know exactly what.

God as First Unmoved Mover

On the basis of these two principles, namely, the principle of causality and the impossibility of an infinite series of causes, some thinkers have argued for the existence of a First Cause or First Mover. It is difficult to avoid the conclusion that there is a First Cause that is uncaused (or First Unmoved Mover) when the argument is properly understood—it is not properly understood through the imagination or any other empirically based mode of thinking, but only through the intellect—one must 'think it', not picture it.

The argument begins with evidence, namely the fact that things move. "Movement" is not limited to any particular kind of movement, such as locomotion; rather, any realization of a potentiality is a change or motion. The argument rests on the principle is that nothing moves itself from potentiality to actuality except by something already in actuality. The reason this principle is undeniable is that nothing can give what it does not have, and what is in potency to an act (or perfection of some kind) does not have that act or perfection—otherwise it would not be in potency to acquire it (what is in potentiality to a perfection of some kind lacks that very perfection).

A thing that has been reduced to motion (from a state of potential motion) depends on a mover (that which possesses the perfection in question and can impart it). Now if something is moving or changing (i.e., a shooting star, a falling leaf, the color of a leaf, etc.,), then the series of movers *in the here and now* that account for the movement cannot extend indefinitely in the here and now (we are not talking about causes extending back into the past).[7] We don't have to account for each mover in the series to know that in the here and now, the series of movers responsible for this movement (i.e., this falling leaf) cannot be infinite. The result of an infinite series of movers is the same as the result of an infinite series of relative factors—one would never achieve a definitive understanding of a relative claim; similarly, nothing would definitively move if each mover is preceded by an indefinite or infinite series of movers.

Many have misunderstood this demonstration because they have attempted to follow it in their imagination, and the imagination is an internal sense, and the act of sensation is subject to time and limited to a material singular that occupies space. This is not an inductive argument that begins with evidence and proceeds to inference to the best possible hypothesis; it is a deductive argument that rests on the principle of causality, which is grounded in the principle of contradiction. To be properly understood, the argument must be kept on the highest level of abstraction. Newton's first law of motion, for example, is understood on the first level of abstraction, not the third level of abstraction that treats of being insofar as it is being. For example, it is true that an object at rest stays at rest and an object in motion stays in motion with the same speed and in the same direction unless acted upon by an unbalanced force (Newton's First Law). There is an agent that initiated the motion, but insofar as the moving thing in space has potentiality, it does not impart to itself that to which it is in potentiality. What then does? Although that is unclear, we do know for certain is that it does not impart to itself what it does not have.

If something is actually moving or changing (not necessarily locomotion or change of place), then it does not give to itself what it does not possess, but receives the perfection it acquires from something that has it, but this latter "something" that has it either has it in itself and did not receive it—which means it was never in potentiality to acquiring it—, or it acquired it—which means it was in potentiality to acquiring it. If the latter is the case, then the sufficient reason for its possessing the perfection in question is outside of it, that is, in another, and so on and so forth. This series of movers either comes to an end or it does not come to an end, in which case the series of movers is indefinite (or infinite). If the series of movers is infinite, then no mover in the series will ever move. In fact, it will be forever waiting to be moved, forever in a state of potentiality to be moved, but it will never acquire actual movement. The change will never be realized.

But the movement has occurred (we saw the falling leaf). Therefore, the series of movers here and now is not infinite, but finite, and if it is finite, there is a first mover, and if there is a first mover, it is unmoved by any prior mover—otherwise it is not first. The first mover is the unmoved mover, which is what others call God. If our reasoning is sound, then at this point we can say that the necessary Being and the first mover are one and the same.

This argument can also be looked upon from a slightly different angle, that is, from the angle of final causes and human motivation. A final cause is an end or purpose; as such, it is a genuine cause of motion. We can ask a student the question: "Why do you bother coming to school?" The answer is typically: "So that I can get my high school diploma". We continue to press the issue: "Why do you want a high school diploma?" "To get into university"; "And why do you want to go to university?" "So I can get a job", is the usual reply. "Why do you want a job?" "So that I can sustain myself and my family"; "Why do you want a family?" Etc. What is interesting to note is that each answer to each question is an end in relation to the previous, but a means in relation to the subsequent end. For example, taking the bus to school every morning is a means to graduating (end), but graduating is a means to university acceptance (less proximate end), and the successful completion of the university program is a means to securing a job (lesser proximate end), etc.

Each end is a genuine moving cause, but if a high school diploma is the reason this person gets up every morning, and a university education is the reason he pursues a high school education, then a university education is the reason for (cause of) his getting up in the morning. Moreover, the prospect of getting a job is the cause of his getting up in the morning, since that is the cause of his wanting to go to university. Furthermore, the desire to sustain himself and his family is the cause of his getting up in the morning, etc. So the question at this point is: "Does the series of causes (ends or final causes) come to an end?" In other words, is the series of final causes indefinite, that is to say, infinite?

Once again, an infinite regress of causes is impossible, for if the series of final causes were infinite, then he would never get up in the morning; he'd be forever potentially out of bed, but never actually out of bed. Hence, the series is finite, and so there is a first cause.

Now although the prospect of having a family is in the distant future (not to mention the job and the successful completion of the university program), this end is exercising, in the here and now, a real causal influence on the person in bed. It is the "reason for" his getting up every morning. The ultimate end of everything we do, of every choice we make, is the first cause of everything we are doing. Socrates rightly saw this ultimate end as happiness, but as far as it goes, happiness is too general a term. What exactly is this "happiness" that is moving or causing us to act? Whatever it is, we know, preconsciously or explicitly, that is has certain properties. Firstly, it is enduring; for no one wants a happiness that, once possessed, is temporary. The reason is that unhappiness does not motivate us, it is happiness that does, so once possessed, we necessarily desire that it remain. Furthermore, that happiness must be free of anxiety, but if that state were to depend on factors outside of our control, such as the stock market or the weather, it would be precarious. And so a property of happiness is that it be sufficient unto itself. Finally, happiness is necessarily an end, not a means, and it is complete— otherwise, it is an imperfect happiness, and it would function as a means to a greater happiness.

Therefore, the first cause, or ultimate end, must be eternal, sufficient unto itself (independent), and complete or perfect. It is necessarily the case that such a first cause exists, because appetite follows upon cognition. If we don't know it, we cannot desire it; if we desire it, then we know it on some level (perhaps confusedly, even preconsciously), and if we know it, then it exists—for we cannot know what does not exist.

That is why Aquinas argues very early on in the *Summa* that human beings possess a natural knowledge of God, albeit a confused knowledge.[8] Any demonstrations of God's existence that he offers later on are clarifications, that is, attempts to bring into focus what is already known naturally, but confusedly and without precision.

A Finite Nonlinear Series

Some people have raised the objection that the series of movers or causes should not be conceived as linear, but geometric if you will, and in that case, we can have a finite series of movers with no first mover—a closed system, if you will. This same objection can be applied to understanding relative claims, so that everything is relative, but the understanding of what is relative depends not on understanding an indefinite linear sequence, but a finite geometric sequence. Thus everything is relative, but understanding can be achieved because we are dealing with a finite geometric series of terms. Hence, there is no need for an absolute; and with respect to motion, there is no need for a first unmoved mover.

It seems to me, however, that this objection cannot avoid the same difficulties outlined above. Consider a closed system of movers, such as one billiard ball moving another, which in turn moves a third, which in turn moves a fourth, etc. This series may continue for a while, but it eventually loops to the point where it began. To make this easier to follow, we'll make one of these billiard balls a solid red, the other a solid blue, the next a solid green, followed by a solid yellow, then a black, and finally a white one. They form not a line, but a circle. We begin anywhere, i.e., the red ball; it moves the blue ball, which in turn moves the green ball. Now if the blue ball, which is moved by the red ball, moves the green ball, then it is true to say that the green ball is moved by the red ball. The green ball in turn moves the yellow ball, which in turn moves the black ball. Using the same reasoning, we can say that the black ball is ultimately moved by the red ball, and the black ball finally moves the white ball. The white ball is moving by virtue of the red ball, at least ultimately. Now the red ball is being moved by the white ball; but the white ball is being moved by the red ball. So the red ball is the mover of the white ball, imparting to the white ball what it is in potentiality to acquiring, but the white ball is imparting to the red ball what it (the red ball) is in potentiality to acquiring. This means that the red ball is both the receiver and the giver of a perfection (i.e., motion) at the same time and in the same respect. The white ball is also the giver and the receiver of the same perfection at the same time and in the same respect.

Each ball in the geometric series is both cause and caused at the same time and in the same respect. In other words, the red ball is the giver of a perfection to the white ball and not the giver of a perfection to the white ball, but a receiver of a perfection from the white ball; and of course the white ball is the giver of a perfection to the black ball, but at the same time not the giver of a perfection to the black ball, but the receiver of a perfection from the black ball. Every mover in the sequence is both mover and moved at the same time and in the same respect, which is contradictory.

And of course the same is true of the series of causes of my definitive understanding of a relative claim, if the series is looked upon as a finite but non-linear series. It cannot depend upon a finite series of relatives, but ultimately on the apprehension of that which is not relative, but absolute.

Finally, some have begun to question the principle of causality on the basis of quantum theory. But this usually results from a univocal understanding of 'causality', that is, understanding causality in terms of mechanics (one particle pushing another particle, etc.). However, the principle of causality is much wider than mechanical causality. That something behaves in a way that cannot be explained using a particular paradigm of causality does not mean it behaves without sufficient reason.

It is in principle impossible to deny the principle of causality, which is rooted in the principle of sufficient reason; for one would have to be omniscient to know that something that we cannot explain simply has no explanation on any level. Furthermore, it is true that some things have no causal explanation, but are merely statistical phenomena; for example, "that incidences of liver cancer are lowest in rural areas". One might look for causes to explain this, such as fresh produce and fresh air, etc., but this may be nothing more than a statistical phenomenon, specifically the law of small numbers. This, however, does not refute the principle of causality any more than it refutes the principle of sufficient reason, for the explanation (the law of small numbers) is sufficient to account for the phenomenon.

9 Primary and Secondary Modes of Being

We have been talking about 'is' (being), its indivisibility, its non-identity with 'non-being', etc. But what does it really mean 'to be'? What are the ways or modes of being? I ask this because it is clear that not everything exists in the same way. What, therefore, is the most fundamental way of existing?

Language reveals a great deal about our pre-scientific understanding of being, for it is 'being' that is given in knowledge. When we come into the knowledge of something, at the very least we can say that 'something is'. But this is true for everything; for example, a hallucination is something, so too is a rainbow as well as an object of the imagination. Is a hallucination a 'being'? It is something, but is it the same kind of thing as what we would normally refer to as a thing? Clearly not; for when we assert that something was a hallucination, we mean that it was not real. So too, an idea 'is', but it is not real—in the sense that it is not outside the mind. I can look for the number five outside my mind, but I will be looking forever, because numbers as such have an existence that is intra-mental, not extra-mental. Numbers exist, but they are not 'real'; all we have outside the mind are discrete multiplicities of things (I can find five apples or five trees, but not the number five in its abstract and universal character).

The word 'real' itself is derived from the Latin word 'res', which means 'thing'. The **primary** mode of being is 'thing' or 'entity', or what we typically refer to as 'substance'. We live in a world of 'things' or substances. Chemistry is the study of the properties and structure of substances; biology is the study of living things;

psychology studies human things, albeit from a very limited angle—focusing, for example, on the behavior of human beings, not their physiology or biochemistry.

There are, however, other modes of being outside the mind that are not primary, but **secondary**, if you will. For example, time does not seem to be a 'thing'; place does not seem to be a 'thing', nor are my 'relations' (i.e., my relation to another as uncle, husband, father, etc.) things in the way that I am a 'thing' or a being. Of course, we cannot deny that place, time, relation, etc., exist merely because they are not things. There are modes of being that exist in a different way, that is, they exist in a way that *depends on* the primary mode of being. Their existence is an "existence in" a thing, such as color, whereas things themselves have a kind of independent existence.

Substance (entity or thing) exercises an existence that is *per se* (exists in itself, not in another). A cat, for example, exists as an independent and delimited entity; a cat does not exist in another, unlike a relation or posture. A substance is a single being. Although a substance is extended into parts, a substance is not identical to its parts, that is, a substance is not identical to its quantity. Rather, a substance 'has' quantity, that is to say, it is subject to quantity, which means it is the subject of quantity. A thing or a substance is the subject of all these other secondary modes of being.

It is important not to visualize any of this—or at least not to allow visualization to become the criterion for understanding; the imagination is more of a hindrance on this level of discussion than it is a help. Some people will imagine "substance" as a kind of avocado pit that underlies the many other secondary modes of being that we will discuss, such as sense qualities. This is a misconception of what substance is in itself. The imagination cannot grasp substance as something separate from its sense qualities; rather, it is distinct from its sense qualities, and the imagination does not make distinctions; it is the intellect that distinguishes.

First, being as such is indivisible, and so if substance or thing is the primary mode of being, substance, insofar as it is 'being', is indivisible. As extended, that is, as quantified, it is divisible (both logically and really). But the extension of a substance is an extension into parts outside of parts (this part is not that part, which is not that part, etc.). A real division of a single substance (not a conglomeration of substances) destroys the thing—cut a cat in half and we no longer have a cat, but two halves of a dead cat.

But a change in quantity is not identical to a change in substance; if we plant a tree and keep an eye on its development, even after a few years we know it to be the same tree, it has not changed in substance, only in quantity—given that we are referring to growth alone. The same is true for every child that becomes an adult. The being itself has not changed absolutely—it is the same person, either your son, or sister, or brother, or spouse—, there is just more of her now than when she was a child.

It is through the intellect that we know "what" things are. Although sense perception is the beginning of knowledge, it does not penetrate to the "what" of things. The "what" or nature of a thing is the intelligible structure or determination of a thing. When that essential determination is apprehended by the mind, it is in the mind as universal (separated from its individuating or material conditions outside the mind).

That essential determination considered in itself, however, is not sensible (one cannot see 'human' or 'feline', or 'canine', etc.).

Quantity or extension into parts outside of parts is a mode of being that is not *per se*, that is, it is not independent, but *exists in* a subject, and that subject is the thing or substance itself. A living organism, for example, is a single being that has a multiplicity of parts that is continuous and heterogeneous (i.e., bone, muscle, nerve tissue, etc.); iron is extended into a multiplicity of parts that is continuous and homogeneous. The living organism is a single being, and its parts are parts of that single being; they inhere in that single subject. This cannot be visualized, only understood, because when we visualize, what we see is nothing but the quantified and qualified (i.e., extended, colored and shaped) thing—only the intellect can distinguish between these modes of being.

It is not quantity that determines a thing or substance to be the kind of thing it is; rather, the substance itself is already a certain kind of thing (i.e., a child, a cat, a plant, salt, etc.); it is the substance that determines the quantity, that is, the parts, to the configuration that those parts possess. For example, there is no pure unintelligible quantity; rather, the parts have an intelligible configuration, such as a hand, or a liver, ears, or cells with a specific number of chromosomes, etc. We speak of human parts, for example, and parts are only intelligible in reference to the whole; for they are parts *of the whole*. Substance is the primary mode of being, not quantity; the specific configuration of the extension is determined by that which is prior, namely the thing itself. What that is specifically will be treated in the chapter that follows.

All knowledge, however, begins in sense perception, and so a material thing will have to possess sensible qualities in order to be known. But quantity as such is not sensible, only potentially sensible. A question about "how much of a thing there is" is essentially different than a question bearing upon a thing's color, or shape, or texture, etc. The former is quantitative, the latter is qualitative. To ask: "Are the apples ripe?" is not to inquire of their quantity. Hence, quality is a different mode of being than quantity, but both are secondary modes of being that "exist in" substance. Quantity and quality are not independent modes of being, but dependent. This means their existence depends on the primary mode of being, which is substance. I cannot find red anywhere in the world, only red things. But qualities presuppose an extended subject; the texture of an apple is other than its extension, but texture, color, and shape, for example, presuppose an extended surface. Thus quantity is prior to quality.

We can distinguish two types of quantity, namely discrete and continuous; the latter being divided into homogeneous and heterogeneous, and we can divide quality into affective qualities (color, odor, texture, etc.), figure or shape, disposition (i.e., flammable), and abilities/debilities (to walk, to run, weakness, vulnerability, etc.).

Other secondary modes of being include where, relation (i.e., things are beside other things, in front of, larger than, or are related by blood, such as brother, mother, cousin, etc., or related by employment, i.e., employee, employer, etc.), when, activity (walking, perceiving, thinking), passivity (being acted upon), posture, and environment (clothed, housed, etc.).

10 Potency and Act: Two Intrinsic Principles of Material Substance

When we ask "what" something is—assuming that it is a real thing, a being in the primary sense—, on a very general level we can say that it is a substance (a thing, an entity). That is "what" it is. As we observe the thing's activity, we come to know "what" it is more precisely—i.e., it is a living organism...it is an animal of some kind, etc. That knowledge is already much more than sense perception. For the object of the sense of sight, for example, is color; each sense faculty has its own formal object (i.e., sound, odor, flavor, pressure, etc.), but the "what" of a thing is not a sensible property. When we apprehend what something is, we are left with an idea that is universal in scope (i.e., plant, dog, human, living thing, inanimate substance, etc.). One cannot visualize the concept "inanimate substance" or "living thing"; one knows through the intellect what it means to be a living thing or an inanimate substance, at least very generally. This knowledge is pre-scientific, and it is this pre-scientific knowledge that is *the condition for the possibility of* a more precise scientific knowledge of the thing. One can only wish to acquire a more precise knowledge of an organism, such as its anatomy or the molecular structure of the cells or the neurophysiology of the brain, etc., on the basis of a pre-scientific knowledge; for it is through this pre-scientific knowledge that one knows, throughout the investigation, what it is that one is studying, namely, a single thing with a multiplicity of complex parts. When one forgets this and begins to substitute this pre-scientific knowledge with a more precise scientific knowledge, one usually ends up making philosophical assertions that are fundamentally absurd.

Imagine if we were reduced to the size of a protein and could go on an expedition inside the human body, perhaps in search of the substance. We'd never find the "substance", because we are already within it; all we see on our expedition are the complex parts of the substance, and parts belong to the category of quantity, and quantity is not substance, but inheres in substance. It is the intellect that apprehends primary being. I do not want to say that sense perception does not apprehend being, because nothing is in the intellect that is not first in the senses, and 'thing' or 'substance' is apprehended by the intellect; what I see and touch when I pick up my pet cat is not pressure, texture, and color, but a substance that is heavy, relatively dense, and black, and can move itself. I know by virtue of intelligence that what I am touching and seeing is a cat, a living sentient substance. A brute animal is also perceiving a cat, but it does not know that it is perceiving a substance, because brute animals do not apprehend what things are essentially.

Potency and Act

Mathematician Rudy Rucker says something interesting that might shed more light on this. He writes:

> A human body changes most of its atoms every few years. Daily one eats and inhales billions of new atoms, daily one excretes, sheds, and breaths out billions of old ones. Physically, my present body has

almost nothing in common with the body I had twenty years ago. Since I feel that I am still the same person, it must be that "I" am something other than the collection of atoms making up my body. "I" am not so much my atoms as I am the pattern in which my atoms are arranged.[9]

The first thing to notice is that Rucker trusts his ordinary pre-scientific knowledge; he knows himself as a single thing, not a multiplicity of parts that are forever in flux. This subjectivity or subjective awareness is a condition for the possibility of knowing things as objects. I know myself as subject when I am knowing something as object; subject and object are correlative terms. I know myself as subject, the tree as object, thus I know immediately that I am not that tree; that tree is an object of my understanding. As a result of this subjective awareness, I know that I am a single being with many parts, and I know from within where my fingers end and where the atmosphere begins, or where the table on which my hand rests begins. Perhaps it is this self-knowledge which is a condition for my understanding that the cat—although it may not know itself as an "I"—is also a single entity or substance, and that its parts end where the litter box or carpet begins.

But this pattern that Rucker speaks of is really something distinct from matter (i.e., the atoms of which he speaks); a "pattern" in relation to matter is determination. To weave a yard into a pattern is to give form or determination to the yarn; thus, matter is related to pattern as indeterminacy or potentiality is related to determination or actuality. A substance is a unity of potentiality and actuality. Every substance is a determinate something. This means that it is actually something that is intelligible (it possesses an intelligible pattern or determination, what Aristotle calls 'substantial form'). But every material substance is also potentially something else; thus, a substance is not a pure unchanging pattern or substantial form, but a composite of potentiality and actuality.

Matter is potentiality, that is, an openness to determination or form. The material cause is always the subject of a change, and a substance or thing can change in two ways: it can change absolutely (i.e., a chemical or substantial change), or it can change relatively (i.e., a physical or accidental change).

A change in relation, or quantity, or quality such as color, for example, are relative modifications of a substance; the substance has not changed absolutely (i.e., a man becomes an uncle, a child grows six inches, etc.). In such changes, it is the substance itself that endures throughout the change.

But a substance can also change absolutely, for example, a cat can die, or iron can change to rust. In other words, one substance changes into a completely different substance with completely different properties.

Now for every change, there is a subject that undergoes the change—otherwise no change has taken place.[10] It is the very meaning of matter to be that enduring subject, because matter is potentiality. Words are the matter of the poet, notes are the matter of a composer, and wood is the matter of a carpenter, etc. Wood, however, is not pure potentiality or pure indeterminacy, because it is actually wood, and wood is an intelligible entity. But wood is only indeterminate in relation to the table that is in the mind of the carpenter, the table he intends to build. But if we burn the wood and change it to a pile of ashes, what is it that has endured throughout the change as the subject of the change? What has endured is the most primary or fundamental potentiality. Matter is potentiality, so the ultimate matter of material substance is pure potentiality or pure indeterminacy.

This pure indeterminacy is not "something", because "something" is a thing, an actuality. It is the potentiality of that something to be something else entirely. This primary matter is the principle of a thing's radical mutability. It does not exist on its own without some sort of essential determination, for it would not, then, be actually anything. It is only known through or with reference to the substantial form of a thing, which is the source or principle of a being's essential intelligibility (to be distinguished from a being's existential intelligibility, the principle of which is the act of existing).

Various Questions

Most people have trouble with this understanding of change, because most people are in the habit of looking upon substance within an 'artifactual' model (or mechanistic model), so to speak. Substances are looked upon as though they were artifacts, which are the sum of their parts. But an artifact is not a "thing" in the primary sense of the word. In ordinary parlance, we speak of a computer, or an automobile, or a calculator, etc., as things. Strictly speaking, however, these are single artifacts, not single beings. An artifact is a number of substances brought together in order to serve a function, usually one that replicates a human function, such as seeing, running, hearing, or throwing, etc. For example, binoculars replicate vision, a motor vehicle replicates locomotion (walking or running), a microphone replicates the power of speech, the computer replicates human computations, the camera replicates sense memory, etc. An alloy is not a single substance either, but a combination of substances, like bronze, which is an alloy of copper, zinc, some other substance, i.e., phosphorus or aluminum. In other words, each substance remains the kind of substance it is in the very coming-to-be of the artifact.

But a human being, for example, is a single substance; every part is of the same kind, that is, every part is human. The nature of the single substance, its essential determination (or essential quality, or substantial form), is found whole and entire in every part—every part of me is human. But a computer does not have a determinate nature, it possesses an artificial form, which is an accidental form in the category of quality. One part of the computer is glass, another part plastic, another part steel, another copper, etc., and all remain what they are, but they are organized into a certain artificial configuration in order to serve a function. An artifact is not essentially one, but many; it is only artificially one (or accidentally one).

I believe these distinctions are important for dealing with the ancient puzzle of the ship of Theseus. Is the ship of Theseus the same ship, after each plank of wood has been replaced over an extended period of time? It seems to me that the difficulty we experience in tackling this problem arises by virtue of a kind of projection: we tend to regard the artifact, such as the ship, or computer, building or automobile, as though it were a single being.

The primary mode of being is substance, and a

substance is one being by virtue of its unique act of existing; an artifact, however, is not a single entity or being. It is an artificial and ordered unity of a number of substances. In short, it is the sum of its parts. What makes the ship "this" ship or the automobile that I purchased "this" automobile—as opposed to the one that some other person purchased (the same make and model)—is "this" matter, not "that" matter, and not the form (the form is the same in both cases). After a small number of the wooden planks that make it up has been replaced, can we say it is the same ship? Similarly, since the day I purchased my first car ten years ago, at various intervals I have had the two doors replaced, the trunk replaced, eventually the hood replaced, the tires, brakes, rotors, driveshaft, transmission, and finally the engine replaced. Can we say this is the same car?

It seems to me that the best answer to this puzzle is that it is "not entirely" the same car. The reason is that the whole artifact is nothing other than the sum of its parts; hence, if the change is not a total change, then the changes are partial, and so the answer to the question ought to be qualified as "partial". If after one year someone were to ask me: "Is that the same car you purchased last year?", my answer is, "Yes it is; I've had to have the passenger door replaced as a result of a small collision, but on the whole it is the same car". "On the whole" means, in this case, "for the most part".

In other words, it is not entirely the same artifact. The following year I'd have to give the same answer: for the most part, it is the same car; for although I've had the trunk and hood replaced, as well as the distributor and camshaft, it is "fundamentally", or for the most part, the same car, but not in its entirety.[11]

Once all the parts have been replaced, I would have to say that this is the same *kind* of car as the original, possibly serving the same purpose, but it is not identical to the original.

What is noteworthy is that this "resulting" car has a unique relation to the original car I purchased that no other car of the same make and model possesses: the original car was the artificial substrate of the changes, the final result of which is this "not-original" car. Indeed, there came a point, not long after it was purchased, at which the original car was no longer there in its entirety, which means only 'parts' of the original were there, more or less, depending on where we are on the continuum of time between the original and the final product.

It seems to me that this becomes more evident when an economic value is placed on the artifact. Consider that I inherited my grandfather's original 1933 Lincoln KB Victoria Coupe, which has a value of around $400,000. Over the years I have made so many replacements that the only thing left of the original is the drive shaft. It is reasonable to expect that the economic value would have decreased significantly, especially given that the replacement parts were made after the year 2000. If this is true, market prices would seem to suggest a lack of identity.

What makes this problem difficult is that an organism is a single being, which is not the same as a single artifact. In fact, if we who consider this problem were not single beings, but merely the sum of a collection of parts, then the original problem of the ship of Theseus would not merely be difficult, it would be simply unintelligible. The principle by virtue of which a material substance—such as a living organism—is "what it is" is intrinsic—the form is in the organism as its principle of essential determination, not on a blueprint in a filing cabinet somewhere; and the principle by virtue of which the substance exists is the act of existing. An organism is not the sum of its parts; rather, the parts of the substance are in the category of quantity, thus they are parts *of the whole*, and these parts can and do change while the substance endures. If I were nothing more than my "parts", I would indeed be a different thing after a number of years of cell replacement—but what then would we make of this enduring "I" of which I am aware? My cells, organs, nerve tissue, etc., are all parts of a single whole, and the whole is prior to its parts, unlike the artifact, whose parts are prior to the whole. These parts can be replaced naturally as occurs in cell replication, but the subject that endures throughout the multiplicity of changes is the single entity.

Another important question that one can ask at this point is whether or not light and empty space are substances. All we can say at this point is that empty space is not nothing; it is something. If between two particles there is nothing, they would be together; if the particles are separated from one another, then something is in between them. If space-time curves, then it is not nothing, but a physical something.[12]

What empty space is precisely, however, is not, it seems to me, a philosophical question, but a scientific one, just as a question bearing upon what a particular chemical is precisely is not a question philosophy can answer. If the question regarding whether or not empty space is a substance is a philosophical question, it is one that, in order to answer it, depends on data supplied by science.

Empty space is certainly not like ordinary things, like water, plants, animals and humans, which are much richer in property. Furthermore, unity is a property of being, but what is a unit of space? If empty space is a substance, at what point is it marked off from another substance? It is much easier to answer this question when it comes to human beings, animals, and plants, but much more difficult to answer when it comes to inert matter. For example, gold is a substance, but is a bar of gold a conglomeration or a unity? A gold or iron bar is a conglomeration of atoms, but an atom is the smallest part of a substance (i.e., gold). At what point can we talk not so much about a part of gold, but the whole of gold? In other words, at what point do we have a single unit of gold? One atom of gold? Or two? Three? Much more difficult is this question with regard to space. Is space one or many?

Whether or not light is a substance is an even more difficult question to answer; but once again, light is something. However, is light a property of space or is it a substance in its own right? I would have to argue, once again, that such a question is, in the end, a scientific question, not a philosophical one, or if it is philosophical, it is one that, in order to answer it properly, depends upon data supplied by science.

Is color a real property of things, that is, a real secondary mode of being? Or is it merely reflected light at different frequencies and wavelengths? There is no doubt that without light, one cannot see the object; it would not be sensible to the sense of sight. Moreover, without a substance or thing to absorb some light and reflect light, we cannot see things, and we see things precisely because they are colored.

But what does it mean for a thing to be colored? It

means a thing is modified in an accidental way, that is, it is a mode of being that inheres in things (i.e., a rose, or an almond, or a peppermint leaf). Reflected light is a necessary condition for seeing an object. But can we not say that a rose is really red, or a peppermint leaf is really green? Is it more correct to say that color is an illusion?

We in fact do say that roses are red and peppermint leaves are green, because that is how we understand it pre-scientifically. It is precisely because we have the power to sense things and things have accidental modes of being, such as color and odor, that we can perceive them, and what we know in the act of perception is something about the being we are perceiving. If there was something wrong with our senses, for example the organ of the eye, we would not know something about the object that is there to know.[13] Language reveals that we understand red or sweet to really be an accidental modification of the apple. Color is a quality of a material thing; that is *what it is*. The color red does not tell me much about the apple, but it does tell me something, namely, that it possesses a certain secondary mode of being, an accidental quality. We can express this, for example, in terms of electromagnetic radiation, but it is only by knowing color through sense perception, actually perceiving colored things, that one knows what color is, and any other additional more precise knowledge of the conditions of color perception is intelligible only on the basis of the original ordinary perception of colored objects. The same is true for our sense of smell—whose conditions are more like color than we once realized (i.e., quantum vibrations).

Thus, to reduce color to electromagnetic radiation would constitute the fallacy of reductionism. The human person can be understood in other terms, for example, in terms of atoms, cells, or complex biological systems, mathematics, etc., but to reduce a human being to such a level is to forget what we know ordinarily and pre-scientifically; it is to forget being, and it is our apprehension of being that is first and remains the condition for the possibility of understanding the thing more precisely and scientifically.

11 First Cause as Being Itself

In chapter four, an *a priori* demonstration of the necessary Being (God) was offered. This was Leibniz' argument, which is the most concise expression of the Ontological Argument first articulated by Anselm. The argument was, essentially, that if a necessary being is possible, then it exists. The reason is that it is a necessary being, and a necessary being cannot not exist. So as long as the necessary Being is not impossible, then the necessary being exists necessarily.

Those who are not persuaded by this argument tend to regard the idea of the necessary Being as a contingent being (a possible being) and then proceed to inquire whether such a being as this actually exists. But the necessary Being is not contingent, but necessary. If such a being is not an impossibility, that is, not logically contradictory (i.e., a square circle), then it exists. If it is possibly the case that it is necessarily the case that p, then it is necessarily the case that p ($\Diamond\Box p \rightarrow \Box p$).

Many students of mine understand this, but find it uncompelling—only a small number find it compelling; instead, most of them find an *a posteriori* demonstration far more satisfying. The following is my own articulation of a demonstration Aquinas propounded when he was approximately 30 years old (Cf. *On Being and Essence*).

Those who reject Leibniz' ontological argument make abundantly clear, in the course of their objections, that knowing "what" something is does not tell us whether or not that something exists. Furthermore, the principle of identity is that 'each being is what it is'; and this is intuitively known. Each being is both a "being" and "what"; the 'what' (nature, essence, or essential determination) of any contingent being is distinct from its existence, which is precisely why knowing 'what' a thing is does not tell us 'whether or not it is'. If the essence and existence of a contingent being were not distinct, it would not be contingent, but necessary—it would be God. A contingent being is one that may or may not exist. We can ask: "What is that thing over there?" The answer is that it is a rhinoceros. That's "what" it is. A rhinoceros is not a necessary being, which means there is nothing in its nature that entails existence; moreover, it can become extinct.

Now a contingent being is "what" it is; but we would not say that a contingent being *is existence*; rather, we would say that it is human, or feline, or canine, etc., and that it "has" existence. Eventually it may not have existence, and it certainly did not always exist. So although 'rational' is part of the essential determination of 'human' (because a human is a rational animal), 'existence' is not part of the essential determination or 'nature' of a contingent being. Whatever is part of the nature of a thing, that is, whatever is included in its definition, will belong to that thing necessarily. For example, 'rational' is part of the nature of man, and so if something is a man, it is necessarily rational (and cannot not be rational). If 'existence' were part of the essential determination of a thing (part of its essence), that thing would exist necessarily and could not not exist—it would not be a contingent being, but a necessary being.

Now contingent beings are beings that may or may not be—they have a possibility of not existing; they 'have' or exercise existence, but they are not existence. It is this distinction between 'what a thing is' and the existence that it 'has' that is critical in coming to understand this demonstration. Once we get a handle on that distinction, we only have to ask the question: "What is the sufficient reason for the very act of existing of a contingent being?" The sufficient reason for the very act of existing is not located in the nature of the thing because 'existence' is outside the essence of the thing, that is, it is not part of its nature (its 'whatness'). If it were, there would be no need to demonstrate the existence of a necessary being, for that would be the necessary Being. Hence, the sufficient reason for its act of existence is not within the nature of any contingent being. In other words, a contingent being cannot sufficiently account for its own act of existence.

But perhaps another contingent being can account for the existence of a contingent being, such as a parent. This, however, is not possible, and the reason is that a thing can only act within the limits of its nature, or within the terms of its essential determination; in other words, it can only do what it has the capacity or power to do; no agent can do what it does not have the power to do—that would be to get something from nothing. It is within the power of a living organism to reproduce, but in order to do so, it must first exist. The sufficient reason for the act of reproduction is within the nature of the organism, but the sufficient reason for the act of existence is not. In other words, the act of existence is prior to activity (it is the act of all acts), and all activity presupposes existence. Things act according to the capacities of their nature, but the act of existence is not included as part of that nature (otherwise, it would be the necessary Being). So although human beings can reproduce, they can only do so on condition that they exercise an act of existing. That is why contingent beings have no dominion over existence; the act of existence is not within their nature, so they don't have the power to impart it. Whatever a contingent being produces presupposes existence—i.e., the existence of the producer and the existence of the matter out of which the product comes to be.

The sufficient reason for the act of existence of contingent beings is outside the nature of every contingent being; hence, the sufficient reason for the very act of existence of each contingent being is to be found in a non-contingent being, a being that does not 'have' an act of existing, but a being that is its own act of existence, a being whose nature or essence is existence. Such a being can impart the act of existing because it is within its nature to do so—that is "what" the non-contingent being is, namely, subsistent being itself. And since whatever belongs to the essence of a thing belongs to it necessarily, this being that is its own act of existing is the necessary Being.

And so the efficient cause of each being's unique act of existing is God, whose nature is to exist. My act of existing is really distinct from my nature, which really exists only because I possess an act of existing; and this is true for every contingent being that exists. Whatever exists has a received existence, except the necessary Being.

It is important to keep in mind that being is always first when considering the coming to be of things in the universe. Prior to being is either being or non-being; if the latter is nothing, then being is first; if the latter is something, then being is first. We cannot ask "what it is?" unless we first apprehend "that it is", but if something 'is', it is a 'what' that is distinct from its existence. Hence, essence follows upon being.

Thus, we can ask the following question: "What is it?" On a very general level, we can say it is an existing material substance. If it is an existing material substance existing outside the mind, it is "what it is" not by virtue of its act of existing—otherwise it would be pure being—, but by virtue of its form (pattern, essential determination), and it is potentially something else by virtue of its matter (its principle of potentiality). A material entity is fundamentally a potency/act unity (it is actually a determinate thing, but potentially something else). The first accidental mode of being of a material substance is quantity, which is extension into parts outside of parts. The parts are not prior to 'thing' or substance, as they are when we consider the coming-to-be of artifacts. A material substance has the parts that it has because it is a material substance of a particular determination, not vice versa; a cat is not a cat because it has cells with 38 chromosomes; it has cells with 38 chromosomes because it is a cat; a human being is what she is not because she has cells with 46 chromosomes; rather, she has cells with 46 chromosomes because she is a human kind of thing. The former would constitute a false major premise in a hypothetical argument ("If an organism has 46 chromosomes, then it is a man" is false; but "If an organism is a man, then it has 46 chromosomes" is true—*caeteris paribus*, and affirming the consequent would be invalid). The parts of a thing are what they are by virtue of the essential determination of the whole (the substantial form), and the potency/act unity which is the substance exists by virtue of the received act of existing.[14]

God as pure being itself, the necessary Being, is the

first existential cause of whatever has existence. Indeed, from nothing comes nothing, but from pure act comes all subsequent act or being. To impart being means to bring something into being from nothing, but that 'nothing' is nothing, not some pre-existing something, and nothing comes 'from' nothing, because nothing is not a terminal "from which" something may proceed; thus, being comes from pure act of being. This, of course, is not to suggest that pure act of being is some sort of "matter" out of which an act of existing is "produced"; that would mean that pure act of being (God) is a kind of potentiality, which is contradictory.

Moreover, not only is God the first existential cause of whatever has being, he is the perpetual or conserving cause of a thing's existence; for just as no contingent being can impart the act of existing either on itself or on another, for the same reason no contingent being can conserve itself in existence; all a living thing can do is preserve its life, but to do so presupposes being (I can't eat and drink—which are activities—unless I am made to be).

A question at this point is whether the above constitutes a natural explanation of the realm of the real or a supernatural explanation. It seems to me that this would depend on what 'natural explanation' means. If the physical universe is the sum total of contingent beings that make it up, then the sufficient reason for the existence of things, the sum total of which is the physical universe, is not found within it, but in that being whose nature is to be. This being, God, is not natural in the sense of being one contingent being alongside other contingent beings; rather, God is supra nature, or supernatural.

However, this being who is being itself is involved in

every natural process, because a thing cannot act or change unless it 'is', and the first and conserving cause of a being's existence is God. This existential causality is not supernatural intervention. What I mean is that there is no nature and no natural processes without God's existential causality, which is first and perpetual. Supernatural intervention is not natural; for example, my body heals itself naturally, not through God's supernatural intervention. This denial of supernatural intervention in the case of my own healing is not a denial of God's existential causality. My body is a real cause of healing, but not a first existential cause. Natural causes can only be natural causes on condition that God existentially causes first, because being is first and God alone is the cause of being—the first and perpetual cause. A supernatural intervention, on the other hand, is what we normally refer to as a miracle.

Can we explain the universe, consciousness, free will, and the evolutionary process without appealing to supernatural intervention? Indeed we can. But we cannot explain the universe, consciousness, free will and the evolutionary process without God's existential causality. There is no evolution without being, and there is no consciousness without being; for consciousness is a certain kind of existing. It follows that there is no natural explanation that is comprehensive without a metaphysical explanation.

But is this metaphysical explanation complete? That would depend on what we mean by complete. I do not know how it is possible to have a complete explanation of reality without each science, and each science is necessarily always open to further development, including metaphysics.[15] Our knowledge of God is indirect and negative (via a knowledge of what God is not); thus, it is forever open to further development and insight. Moreover, our knowledge of another human person is always incomplete, let alone our knowledge of God. If God were to choose to reveal himself in a way that cannot be ascertained through the indirect and negative method of human reasoning, but directly, that revelation would certainly complete the natural, which implies that the natural knowledge of God and his relationship to the universe is incomplete; but our understanding of that revelation would have to remain incomplete insofar as God is infinitely knowable and human intelligence is limited.[16]

Further Thoughts on Chance

Earlier we inquired whether chance, which is a disorder, could possibly be, on another level, something ultimately ordered. Chance is essentially relative, and as such it can only be understood in relation to something other than it, namely, a series of events ordered to an end. In relation to these series of ordered events, chance is a disorder. But is it possible that these disorders are, ultimately, ordered occurrences?

From the point of view of the first cause, it would seem that nothing can be a chance occurrence. The reason is that God's knowledge is the measure of what 'is', and what 'is' includes beings and their acts (activity is, occurrences are, including chance occurrences). Nothing is unforeseeable to God, so in their aspect of unforeseeability, chance occurrences are impossible from the point of view of the first cause.

But does that mean that every chance occurrence from our point of view, has an absolute significance? We've all experienced chance occurrences that turned out to be the beginnings of something profoundly significant, i.e., a relationship that resulted in a marriage, or a job opportunity, which led to another thing, which in turn led to something else, etc., such that when we look back, we are tempted to conclude that this or that intersection could not have been purely coincidental, but intended by God.

Such occurrences can indeed be both a matter of chance and a matter of providence; chance is a real but relative disorder, but not an absolute disorder—for order must be prior to disorder, since disorder depends upon order to be intelligible. Nor does this mean that every chance intersection carries the same weight of significance. Its significance for me might be much less for another, and it might be less significant for both us than another chance occurrence.

What would it mean to say that everything is governed by laws of randomness? As was said earlier, randomness need not be the same as chance; the former is ordered, intelligible, and can be the object of study; its intelligibility can be expressed mathematically. The tools of statistics enable us to tame randomness, to some degree at least, and with no guarantees—for it is ultimately an order that is too large for us to manage. Randomness can only occur in an ordered universe, an order too large for the mind to manage completely. So whatever it means to say that the universe is governed by randomness, it does not mean that ultimately the universe is not governed by an intelligent first cause.

12 Some Implications of God as Being Itself

God is that being whose nature is identical to his existence, and God's nature is to exist. It follows that God cannot not exist; he is necessary. The beginning of the *a priori* argument of Leibniz is the end of Aquinas's *a posteriori* argument.

A number of things follow from the above. First, it follows that God is one. There cannot be two necessary beings, because there cannot be two beings that are "being itself". All we have to do is ask what it is that would distinguish the one from the other? It would have to be something outside of what they are in common. But what are they? They are being itself, that is, two beings whose essences are to be. But outside of being itself is non-being (nothing). Hence, nothing distinguishes them, and so they are not "they" (plural), but one.

It also follows that if God is his own act of existing, then God is pure act. What this means is that his essence or nature is not in potentiality to existence, as is the nature of a contingent being; his nature is his act of existence. Thus, God is pure act of existing without any admixture of potentiality. But matter is potentiality. Therefore, God is not a material being.

Nor is God extended, because material beings are extended. Furthermore, God does not possess any accidental modifications, like color, where, shape, habits, etc., for if God is pure act of being, he is not in potentiality to any kind of modification. Quantity or extension is an accidental modification of a being. Hence, God is not a quantity.

Looked at from another angle, the necessary Being, who is being itself, cannot be divided into two, and to be a quantity is to be divisible, either logically or really. Being pure and simple cannot be divided into parts; consider what that would mean, this part of God is not that part of God. But if this part of God is being, then there cannot be anything outside of that part, for outside of being is non-being, which is nothing. If there are no parts outside of this part, then there is no "this part". This part is so only so in relation to that part. Hence, there are no parts in God. Also, the word 'divisible' means potentially divided. Since God has no potentiality, God is not divisible; thus he is not a quantity.

Moreover, if God has no potentiality, God does not change, because change is the realization or actualization of a potentiality.

It can also be inferred deductively that God is not subject to time; for time is the measure of movement according to a before and an after. But God does not move, for he does not change, because change is the realization of what is in potentiality towards a perfection. But that being who is his own act of existing cannot be in potentiality to anything; for there is no potentiality in God, and God is the first existential cause of whatever is. Furthermore, whatever perfection exists, God is the existential cause of it, and so he cannot lack it if he is its source.

Hence, God is eternal. And what is eternal is not something that endures indefinitely throughout time; rather, what is eternal is simply present without a before and an after. In other words, God is intimately present to every moment of human history simultaneously; there is no future and no past with God, only the present.

Furthermore, God is not in place, therefore God is not *in* the universe nor outside of it. To be *in* place requires quantity and figure. God has no quantity, therefore he is nowhere in particular, but present to everything that is, more intimately than anything else can be present to something. For if God alone imparts the act of existing on contingent beings, then God is intimately and immediately present to anything that has being. Hence, there cannot be anything between God and a contingent being. Therefore, wherever there is something, God is more intimately and immediately present to that something than anything else could possibly be.

But is the necessary Being, who is being itself, intelligent? Is the necessary Being a person (of a rational nature)? Consider that a thing is known in so far as it is in act—to the degree that it is in potency (indeterminate), it is unintelligible. Now knowledge is in us; so when I know something, i.e., that cat, what I know exists in me in some way. It does not exist in me materially, but immaterially. When I know the nature of a thing, that nature exists in my mind as a concept or idea. The intellect abstracts the essential determination from the material conditions of the thing—which is why the idea of the nature of that thing exists in the mind as a universal idea (it is not restricted by matter). The potential intellect (in potentiality to that essential determination, or in potentiality to knowledge of the thing) becomes actualized by that essential determination (the mind becomes what it knows in an immaterial way). Knowledge, at least in part, is precisely that: the mind becomes the essential determination of the thing that exists physically outside the mind (knowledge is a unity between knower and known). So a thing is known insofar as, in the mind, it is in act. If God is pure act (or pure actuality, or pure act of existing), then God is perfectly intelligible to himself. Moreover, act is perfection, for a thing is perfect in so far as it is in act. But God is pure act of existing, therefore God is perfect, and if God is perfect, he cannot lack any perfection—otherwise he would be in potency to further act. Now, of all the perfections found in beings, intelligence is considered preeminent; for intellectual beings are more powerful than those without reason. Therefore, it follows that God is intelligent; hence, he is a person.

However, God does not possess knowledge as we do; for knowledge in us is a perfection that is acquired. God's knowledge, rather, is identical to his act of existence; for God is entirely simple, that is, entirely without composition. There is nothing in God that is distinct from his existence. If God's knowledge were distinct from his existence, there would be composition in God, and thus potentiality in God. Now, there is nothing outside of God's act of existing, since God is pure being itself. Hence, God's knowledge is his Being. Also, if there was knowledge in God, and this knowledge was not his act of existing, then it would be related to his act of existing as potency is related to act. But there is no potentiality in God, as was shown above. Hence, God's knowledge is his existence.

It also follows that any other perfections, such as love, justice, wisdom, power, beauty etc., are found in God, but they are identical to his existence for the reasons stated above.

Moreover, God is infinitely knowable, because he is being pure and simple, without the limitations of an essence distinct from his act of existing. He is therefore incomprehensible; He is the unutterable mystery that can never be completely understood or circumscribed by a finite intelligence.

Now good is a property of being, and so if God knows himself, who is pure being and thus pure goodness, it follows that he necessarily loves himself. For the good is that which all things desire, and all things desire first and foremost their own perfection, that is, their own act.

If God is pure act without any admixture of potentiality, then God is unlimited Good—for potentiality is the source of limitation in things. What is supremely Good without limits is, if known, necessarily loved.

Also, God's willing and God's knowing is not a power or potency that can be actualized. God's knowing and willing are eternally act, for his willing and knowing are identical to his act of existing. So God always knows himself and loves himself. He imparts existence to contingent beings not out of necessity, but through his own will. Whatever is, he knows, for it is his knowledge and will that cause other things to be. Hence, God does not learn as we learn, God does not discover as we discover. God does not move from potentiality to actuality, that is, from potential knowledge to actual knowledge. Hence, anything that is, exists by virtue of God's knowledge and will. If God does not know it, it does not exist.

If God's knowledge is his existence, then it follows that God's knowledge is the cause of whatever has being. A thing exists because God knows it (and of course wills it into being). Existing things exist independently of our knowing them, but this is not the case for God. Whatever exists, exists because he knows it. Real being is the measure of man's mind, but God's mind is the measure of the real.

Since God is the first existential cause of whatever has existence, it follows that God has complete dominion over being. We might have dominion over the fish, the animals, the trees, etc., but we do not have dominion over being. We cannot impart being (bring something into being from nothing). Now, since there is nothing outside of being, and God has dominion over being, it follows that he is unlimited in power.

If God is his own act of existing, then it follows that God is infinite (without limits). In other words, he does not have a nature that is distinct from his act of existing that limits that act of existing. Hence, God is without limits (infinite).

Also, whatever is, is good; in other words, good is a property of being. Thus, to exist is good; that is why things struggle to perpetuate their existence. Evil is a lack of due being, a lack of something that should be there. And so it follows that if God is his own act of existing, then God is supremely Good, or perfect Goodness, or Goodness without limits. It would seem to follow that God cannot do or will evil; whatever God does is good insofar as he does it.

Furthermore, if God is omnipotent, and if God is Goodness without limits, then it follows that everything is under the providential hand of God, so to speak. A human person has the choice not to love God and not to trust in his providence, but those who do love God have the assurance that whatever happens to them in their lives is permitted by God ultimately for their greatest good. Omnipotence means that God can do whatever he wills, and perfect goodness implies that he wills only what is best. The two together imply that God wills our greatest good and is able to bring it about—if we allow him to do so. Hence, whatever he allows to happen to us in our lives is permitted by him, ultimately for our greatest good if we choose to love him—this, of course, is not to suggest that God does not love those who do not choose to love him.

Every perfection that exists in God is identical to his act of existing. Beauty is a perfection, and the properties of beauty seem to be integrity, harmony, and radiance or intelligibility. It follows that God is subsistent Beauty. Hence, whatever is beautiful, such as a beautiful sunset, beautiful scenery, the beauty of the stars, a beautiful face, or the beauty of a mathematical equation, etc., is an imperfect reflection of God's perfect and infinite beauty. And if the human person has a natural desire to behold the beautiful, he has a natural desire to see God.

Justice is a perfection (an unjust man is not regarded as a perfect man), therefore, in God, justice is identical with his act of existing. Thus, God is justice. Hence, we can conclude that ultimately, injustice is temporary. God cannot allow injustice to endure. Nor is it possible for God to ever be unjust.

Truth is the conformity between what is in the mind and what is (in reality). But what is, exists by virtue of being known by God and being willed into existence (as we said above). God's knowledge is the measure of reality, not vice versa. God is thus the measure of truth. Therefore, God does not possess the truth, rather God is Truth. And so it follows that whoever loves truth, ultimately loves God, just as whoever loves justice—and not everybody does—, such a one ultimately loves God.

The object of the will is "the good". Thus, whatever is willed is regarded as good. Now the very fact that I am moved to love the good without qualification constitutes my natural knowledge and love of God, who is goodness itself without qualification. I do not see God as he is in himself, but I am inclined to him in my every inclination, that is, in every good that I pursue. What I seek in the pursuit of every good is ultimately the good without qualification. Now I cannot desire what I do not know, so on some level, I must know that such a good exists. From another angle, I naturally will to know the causes of things, and that search will never end until I know the ultimate cause.

I naturally will a happiness that is unqualified, enduring, and sufficient unto itself. The only good that corresponds to such a description is the supreme good, who is goodness itself. Again, I could not desire such a good unless I know that it exists, on some level at least. And so this life is a search for God.

Joy is the state that results from the satisfaction of the will, which is the possession of the good. Now, if God's goodness is his act of existence, and if the object of the will is the good, then to see and know God as he is in himself is to experience the perfect satisfaction of the will, which is joy. And since we don't see the supreme Good directly while in this earthly state, it follows that the joy of knowing God as he is in himself is simply unimaginable. To possess that joy eternally would be "heaven".

Finally, love means to will the good of another (benevolence), and goodness is a property of being. Hence, to exist is basically good. God's act of creating (bringing things into being) is an act of love, that is, a willing that the goodness of existence be enjoyed by the creature. Now, man is an intelligent being whose highest activity is to know and to love. Therefore, man's highest and greatest possible achievement is to know and love God. It follows that it is reasonable to spend every ounce of one's energy towards the attainment of that goal. A reasonable life is one directed ultimately towards the possession of God in knowledge and love.

13 God and Free-Choice

If God is the first existential cause of all that is, and my free-choices 'are', then does it not follow that God is the first cause of my choices? The simple answer is, yes. No contingent being is the first existential cause of anything, so I am not the first cause of my free-choices; God is.

This, of course, seems contradictory. If God creates my free-choices, then it would seem free-choice is merely an illusion. Or worse, God creates moral evil.

This is probably the most difficult problem in the philosophy of being; what follows is my attempt to shed some light on it.

I am aware from within that I responsible for the choices that I make. In other words, I know from within that my choices are self-determined. What this means is that I am aware of alternatives to choose from, and each alternative contains limited goods that other alternatives do not contain, and vice versa. If any alternative contained all the goods that each of the other alternatives contained individually, then there would be nothing over which to deliberate; the choice would not be free, but determined beforehand to that alternative. But no alternative contains all the goods that each of the others contains individually, which is why I deliberate (I could attend this university, which has an excellent mathematics department, but a weak athletics program; I could attend that university, which has an excellent athletics program, and only a good mathematics department, etc.). I cut off the deliberation process at some point (my will commands the intellect to stop deliberating), and in doing so, I determine myself to a particular alternative. Free choice is precisely that self-determination process.

Now I have the power to deliberate in this way because the intellect is an immaterial power.[17] Just as I apprehend being without qualification, I also apprehend the good without qualification. The senses cannot perceive a general idea or understand a general course of action, but the intellect does apprehend general ideas that cannot be sensed, such as "generality", "quantity", "indivisibility", etc., and the intellect can understand a general course of action (i.e., to be a good person not just now, but always; to always seek justice, etc.). The mind understands being as such, and since good is a property of being, the mind understands the good as such. In fact, the mind understands the good without qualification because the intellectual creature wills the good without qualification; for the will never finds rest in finite goods.

I can say to someone: I will love you always, forever, no matter what, etc. That is an unqualified love. It zeros in on a particular person, but I will her good without any qualifications or conditions—whether I remain steadfast in that love is another matter. That decision to "love this person always, forever", etc., is either a delusion on my part, or it is a real possibility. The very idea of loving someone forever and always is itself testimony to our ability to transcend the limitations of matter. One cannot sense forever and ever—a purely sentient creature has no idea of such a thing, for there is no sensation that corresponds to it; but the mind does apprehend this idea, as is obvious from a small sampling of a variety of love songs. That a person is able to commit to such a thing implies an appetite that is not material or inextricably tied to the senses, as are the sense appetites. The objects of the sense appetites are sensible goods apprehended by the senses, and thus limited by matter to a particular 'this' or 'that' (i.e., this piece of meat). An animal limited to sense cognition cannot be moved to desire the good of another for the other's sake, forever and ever, for the sense appetites lack such extension. Only an appetite that transcends matter can carry out such a commitment, and such an appetite is the will (the rational appetite). The failure to carry out that commitment testifies not so much to the impossibility of such an idea or commitment as it does to the weakness of the will, the free choice in favor of an alternative that is sensibly more pleasing than the good of the other.

But this is precisely the kind of entity that God has brought into existence and sustains in existence, namely a being that can apprehend the good as such and will the good without qualification. I will your good, not for what you do for me, but rather as though you were another me. I choose this alternative or not, but I can only do so on condition that I exist and am maintained in existence. Thus, I determine myself, and I am a real cause of my own course of action, but I am not the first existential cause, only a real but secondary cause.

Free-choice is the determination by the self to an alternative that contains finite goods that are incommensurable, but this presupposes that my will is moved to the good without qualification (I am not determined to a particular good), and in this I have no free choice. Moreover, since nothing moves itself from potentiality to actuality except by something already in actuality, I depend on God to move my will to the good without qualification. God can do so without determining my will to this or that alternative; thus, I have no free will, only free-choice. Whatever any contingent being moves, it determines (i.e., if I move a piece of chalk, I determine its place). God alone can move the will without determining it; his efficient causality is not limited in a way that the agency of a contingent being is limited. God knows what it means to move the will without determining it, and he can will into existence a being whose will he moves without determining it to this or that alternative.

It is this being that, after deliberating over alternatives, determines himself or herself to a particular alternative; and it is the will that commands the intellect to cut off all further deliberation. The choice that is made is the last alternative deliberated over before the will made its command, and if that alternative is the most deficient morally, then I am the first deficient cause of my choice (while God is the first cause of whatever being there is to my action); thus I am the first cause of the evil or deficiency that belongs to the alternative: i.e., I chose the option of lying under oath rather than telling the truth and paying the price of doing so, etc. Since good is a property of being and evil is a lack of due being, God is the first cause of whatever goodness there is in an evil action, while the moral agent is the first cause of the lack that ought not to be, insofar as he or she freely chose an alternative that was morally lacking and thus forbidden.

God is not limited by any contingent being, so not only is he able to move a being to the good without qualification without determining that being to this or that course of action, God can also choose not to allow the entire result of man's choices to derail his ultimate purpose in creating the universe. For nothing determines God, who is pure act of being—God is truly

91

unlimited. Whatever evil choices human beings make, that is, whatever morally deficient alternatives they might determine themselves to, God who is unlimited in knowledge, whose knowledge is the measure of what is, and who is unlimited in power because he has complete dominion over being, can choose not to allow the totality of that evil to have the final word, so to speak, that is, to hinder the overall plan of providence.

14 Being and Logic

We've said many times over that being is first—prior to being is nothing—, and it is being that is given in knowledge. Whenever I know anything at all about anything, at the very least I know that it is, and unless I first know that it is, I cannot know anything more specific. That is why metaphysics, and not epistemology, is first philosophy. And if the philosophy of being is first philosophy, then logic has its roots ultimately in the principles of metaphysics.

The principle of identity, for example, is presupposed in every logical argument, whatever form the argument may take, that is, whether we are talking about a hypothetical syllogism, a categorical syllogism, a modal argument, or an inductive argument, etc. For example, "All men are rational; John is a man; therefore, John is rational", presupposes that each being is what it is: a man is a man, not a flower. Or, consider the following argument: "If it is possibly the case that it is necessarily the case that p, then it is necessarily the case that p" ($\Diamond\Box p \rightarrow \Box p$). Unless each being is what it is, not what it is not, it is not possible to determine that p is necessarily the case (i.e., a triangle is necessarily three-sided, not four-sided).

An invalid argument violates the rules of logic, but the rules of logic are not conventions or the result of a majority vote taken at one time. They are rooted in the laws of being, in particular the principle of contradiction, which follows upon the apprehension of being; moreover, it is from the principle of contradiction that the principle of causality is derived, and it is the middle term that is the cause of an argument's conclusion. Consider the following:

All socialists favor more social legislation
The entire Liberal cabinet favors more social legislation.
Therefore, the entire Liberal cabinet is socialist.

The conclusion is not contained in the premises, thus it is not possible to draw this conclusion with certainty. The conclusion, in other words, lacks necessity; it is a *non-sequitur*. But what lacks necessity lacks being, because necessity arises from being (whatever exists necessarily exists, as long as it exists). In other words, what lacks necessity lacks determination—pure possibility, or pure indeterminacy, is not actually anything.

The middle term in the above argument—which is the cause of the conclusion—is undistributed: for although it is true that all socialists favor more social legislation and that the entire Liberal cabinet favors more social legislation, it is left undetermined whether all those who favor more social legislation are socialists. Is it possible to favor more social legislation without being a socialist? In other words, is favoring more social legislation a sufficient condition for being a socialist? Or is it merely a necessary condition?

It is indeed possible to favor more social legislation without being a socialist; the former does not determine a person to the latter. Hence, the conclusion above remains indeterminate (unknowable given the premises alone). The middle term does not have what it takes to cause the conclusion, and so what is happening in the conclusion is that one is deriving determination from indetermination; in other words, one is taking more from less, or deriving something from nothing. But from nothing comes nothing, not something.

Undistributed means unfinished, or incomplete; so an undistributed term is not entirely determined. Hence, the meaning is incomplete, as an unfinished motion is incomplete. If a man is driving to the city of Toronto, then Toronto is the term of his motion, and it is the terminal that terminates the motion, rendering it intelligible. "All giraffes are animals", but this proposition leaves undetermined whether all animals are giraffes. It is possible that not all animals are giraffes; the species has a greater determination than the genus. In short, to try to derive determination out of indetermination is to try to get something from nothing, that is, to get act from potency.

Similarly, a distributed term in the conclusion that is not distributed in the premises—the violation of another rule—is to get something from nothing. For example,

All teenagers are familiar with the difficulties of being young.
No adult is a teenager.
Therefore, no adult is familiar with the difficulties of being young.

It is impossible to derive the conclusion from the given premises, because the major premise leaves "those familiar with the difficulties of being young" undetermined or unfinished. In other words, the meaning of the proposition is unfinished, it is incomplete, and it is precisely this indeterminacy that leaves us in the dark about whether all those who are familiar with the difficulties of being young are teenagers. In other words, we need more information before we are able to come to that determination; the motion or meaning of the proposition is not terminated. However, every agent acts for an end, and every proposition is meaningful to the degree it terminates (a motion becomes increasingly intelligible as it approaches its end), and it is obscure to the degree that it has yet to be further determined.

A conclusion with a distributed term that is undistributed in the premise is similar to the proposition that "all those vehicles heading in the direction of Montreal are going to Montreal". The conclusion cannot be determined on the basis of what is indeterminate; for that would be to derive something from nothing (there are many possible terminals on the way to Montreal, I.e., Kingston, Brockville, Ottawa, etc.).

It is precisely this underdetermination that characterizes inductive arguments. The scientific method is grounded in the logic of induction, which is why a hypothesis put forth as an explanation of the evidence requires testing. The antecedent of the major premise of a hypothetical argument is, when unknown, a hypothesis. The minor premise is simply a piece of evidence, which is all we have initially. That evidence, in the major premise, is the consequent.

If (hypothesis$_{1, 2, 3, 4, \text{or} 5, \text{etc.}}$), **then you will have a fever.**
You have a fever.
Therefore, (hypothesis$_{1, 2, 3, 4, \text{or} 5, \text{etc.}}$).

To settle upon a hypothesis simply on the basis of the evidence, which is the consequent, is unwarranted, at least from the point of view of deductive reasoning. But that is precisely why the hypothesis requires testing; and of course every scientists knows this. That is why it is especially ironic that a scientist would claim that one can derive more from less (as some physicists have done), or that the effect can be greater than the cause, or that an occurrence has taken place without a cause (or sufficient reason). If that were possible, then determination can be derived from indeterminacy, and one would not need to test one's conclusions; for the condition that moves us to test our hypotheses is precisely the recognition that an underdetermined conclusion is uncertain and thus requires further determination. A probable conclusion is not a certain conclusion. To claim that something can be derived from nothing (or that more can be derived from less) is to claim that certainty can be derived from uncertainty, or necessity from probability.

To confuse necessary and sufficient conditions is to confuse determinacy with indeterminacy. And so without the principles of determinacy and indeterminacy, or actuality and potentiality, logic becomes impossible.

15 Thoughts on Knowledge and Reality

If all knowledge begins in sensation, then knowledge begins with the particular (the individual, the concrete evidence, etc.). It would seem, then, that all knowledge is fundamentally inductive; moreover, since the conclusion of an inductive argument is only probable, not certain, it would seem that knowledge is fundamentally uncertain.

It is indeed true that "nothing is in the intellect that is not first in the senses"; thus, all knowledge begins in the realm of the particular. It does not follow, however, that nothing is certain. The first act of the intellect is simple apprehension, or what some thinkers have referred to as "abstractive induction". The object of this act is the essential intelligibility of a being, that is, its "whatness" or nature, which is general, not particular. The second act of the intellect is existential judgment, by virtue of which one apprehends the existential intelligibility of a being, that is, its existence; and finally, the third act of the intellect is reasoning, which is both deductive and inductive.

Abstractive induction (the first act of the intellect) is different from inductive reasoning. The latter presupposes abstractive induction. One cannot reason inductively unless one knows "what" one is talking about, that is, unless one possesses general ideas in the first place. We cannot begin to determine the probability of schizophrenia given the evidence $[P(H/E)]$, or the probability of specific symptoms given that a person does not have schizophrenia $[P(E/H_0)]$, unless one first knows what "schizophrenia" is, or what an "illness" is, or what "evidence" is, or what "probability" is, etc. And that is just what "abstractive induction" is; the first act of the intellect which apprehends the "whatness" or general nature of a thing.

The mind is an immaterial power, and what it does first is it abstracts the "essential determination" (i.e., the essence of the thing or action or relationship, etc.) from all its individuating conditions in the phantasm. The mind conceives that intelligible content (the concept or idea) of a being, abstracted from its individuating conditions, which is why it is universal in the mind, while outside the mind it is a particular instance of 'tree', or 'man', or 'justice', or a particular instance of a 'certain kind of argument', etc.

Existential judgment, the second act of the intellect, occurs simultaneously, and it is the apprehension of the very act of existence of the being before me. I know "what" you are through abstractive induction, but at the same time I apprehend "that you are" (that you exist) through a distinct act of the intellect, which is existential judgment. Considered in itself, abstractive induction (or simple apprehension) is incomplete; it is perfected in the act of existential judgment. Abstractive induction grasps "a potentiality for existence"—because an 'essence' is a potentiality for existence—, while through existential judgment I immediately apprehend that this being before me is more than "what it is" essentially; in other words, the act of existing of this being does not add anything to the nature of this being, that is, it does not change it specifically in any way; rather, it adds an existential actualization. I know what it is, but I also know something more, namely, "that it is", and the intelligible content of this apprehension is not a concept (it is not an essence), but it is an intelligibility other than the intelligibility of the "essence"; it is an existential intelligibility that is the perfection of the "whatness" that I apprehend in the first act of the intellect, namely the intelligibility of its existence.

These two acts of the intellect are the conditions for the possibility of the more complex acts of reasoning. By virtue of those first two acts of the intellect, we can now reason deductively, for example, we know that "All men are rational", and we judge that this being is a man; therefore, we conclude that "this being is rational". We also reason inductively; for we know that 87% of students in this school are East Indian, and so we conclude that this person, a student of this school, is East Indian. This latter conclusion is a valid inductive argument, which means that it is reasonably probable. Similarly, 78% of the apples in this orchard are grade A; therefore, 78% of all the apples in this orchard are grade A. The conclusion is reasonably probable on condition that the sample is large enough and is representative. Both kinds of inductive arguments presuppose a more fundamental kind of induction, namely simple apprehension. Nicholas Rescher argues:

> And fortunately, a case-by-case determination is not generally needed to validate generalizations. We can establish claims about groups larger than we can ever hope to inventory. Recourse to arbitrary instances, the process of indirect proof by reduction *ad absurdam*, and induction (mathematical and scientific) all afford procedures for achieving generality knowledge beyond the reach of an exhaustive case-by-case check….Finite knowers can, of course, know universal truths. After all, we must acknowledge the prospect of inductive knowledge of

general laws, and we will have it that a knower can unproblematically know—for example—that "All dogs eat meat." But what finite knowers cannot manage is to know this sort of thing in detail rather than at the level of generality.[18]

Knowledge is, generally speaking, difficult to achieve. Knowledge of the most important things in life, however, seems to be much easier to acquire. For example, what could be more important than knowing that God, who is eternal, omniscient, omnipotent, supremely good, etc., exists? And yet proving that the necessary Being exists is simpler than proving anything else: "If the necessary Being is possible, then it exists." Although most people might not have thought of that nor even find the argument compelling, it can be argued that people naturally believe in God through a rapid reasoning process that is for the most part preconscious, a reasoning process that begins with an intuitive knowledge of the principle of causality and the impossibility of an infinite regress of causes.

After the knowledge of God, what can be more important than knowing the fundamentals of what is morally right and wrong? And yet the basic principles of practical reason are naturally known intuitively and from within; for every human being has a natural inclination to preserve his life, as well as a natural inclination to know, to contemplate, to engage in intelligent play, to socialize, to beget life, to situate oneself within a community, and to seek harmony between oneself and some totally 'other' source of meaning, and to try to bring about harmony within the complex elements of the self. All these are human goods that together constitute human well-being.

Combine this with our natural understanding that "good is to be done and evil is to be avoided"—no one disagrees with this, only with what specifically counts as good and evil—and the stage is set for unravelling the logical implications of these principles, for example, one ought not to harm others, one ought to revere the marriage bond, to love truth, to treat others as you would like to be treated, etc.

Knowledge becomes increasingly difficult to achieve as we descend to lower levels of abstraction—this too is where ethics becomes somewhat more complicated, requiring more distinctions, more specific principles, and greater attention to details. But it is here, at the lowest levels of abstraction, that most of our day to day reasoning takes place, and on this level, our reasoning for the most part proceeds from the effect to the cause, and there are often a vast number of possible causes (hypotheses) that account for the same effect. The result is that many of our conclusions have only a degree of probability, and thus require testing.

This is the kind of reasoning that characterizes those sciences that take place on the first level of abstraction, such as biology, chemistry, physics, psychology, etc., as well as those areas of study that are not abstract at all, such as history, or reasoning about the meaning of everyday occurrences, the gestures of others, the significance of people's moods, the truth of the news we read about, etc. The reason for this difficulty in acquiring knowledge has to do, once again, with indeterminacy (potentiality). A necessary condition is not a sufficient condition; for example, a fever is a necessary condition for having the flu (as opposed to the flu vaccine), but not a sufficient condition. Sufficient conditions have greater determination. If one does not know the sufficient condition, one cannot determine it from a knowledge of a necessary condition. Necessary conditions, unless they are simultaneously sufficient, have a greater degree of indeterminacy than sufficient conditions. Although a person has a fever, it cannot be determined on that basis alone that he has the flu.

More specifically, the difficulty in acquiring knowledge can be attributed to a kind of intelligence that is profoundly limited by matter. In other words, potentiality (or indeterminacy) is the source of this difficulty, both on the side of the knower and on the side of the object known.

On the side of the knower, knowledge is limited by place, time, and sense perception: "Nothing is in the intellect that is not first in the senses" (peripatetic axiom). More specifically, knowledge begins with a question. The word itself is from the Latin verb *quaerere*, which is "to quest" or "to seek", or "to journey". Note the expression "to pose a question" (from Old French *poser*: "to set, place, put"). To pose is to position oneself, as we do when we pose for a picture; it is a spatial verb, for when we position or set ourselves, we do so facing a particular direction, and when we face one direction (i.e., north), we do so to the exclusion of another direction (i.e., south and south west and south east, etc.). I cannot perceive a group of people all at the same time; as I focus on one person, I do so at the expense of a precise perception of another. In other words, as I focus on this person, others are in the periphery, and although I can perceive them, my perception lacks precision. But as I begin to shift my attention and focus on another person before me, the previous perception loses precision and the object of my new perception gains a precision that was lacking a moment ago. When we pose a question, we position ourselves for a quest. In other words, to ask a question is to pursue a line of inquiry.

Note the spatial undertone surrounding the very idea of "questioning". Human knowing, although it is not reducible to sense perception, shares in the limitations that sense perception imposes, and of course all knowledge begins in sensation. The human person is situated in place; for he is corporeal. Furthermore, we only come to know "what things are" (their natures) through their activities, which is why coming to understand the natures of things is slow and gradual. But some people observe the activity of things from one angle, while others from a different angle. Most importantly, the angle is determined by the particular questions posed, and questions are rooted in specific interests and problems. Some people are interested in one kind of problem to solve, while others are interested in problems of a different kind. Some seek more precision (science), because they are interested in solving certain problems that require a very precise understanding of how something works; others show interest in a more general knowledge in order to proceed in another direction, such as a better understanding of the nature of the human person or the overall purpose of human life, or the nature of knowledge, as opposed to how the brain works.

Our access to the real is through the subjective—it is a knowing subject that knows real things, a subject who is situated in a particular place at a particular time and who is confronted with a task to be done, which in turn gives rise to specific problems to solve.[19] If we fail to appreciate the role that subjective epistemic conditions play in the genesis of our knowledge, we may end up believing that the epistemic model or conceptual framework through which we see and interpret the real is more comprehensive than it actually is—it is profoundly limited and is continually developing.

When a person zeros in on specific aspects of reality, other aspects are easily overlooked; for when we pursue a line of inquiry, aspects of reality that we encounter along that road are opened up to us, while alternative lines of inquiry and the aspects of the real that they open up are closed to us, just as attention to specific tasks can blind us to things that are right in front of us.

Two questions bearing on the same object but posed from slightly different vantage points and rooted in slightly different interests will open up two lines of inquiry that in due time and after some distance will have diverged significantly from where they were initially. A slight turn on a road can lead one into an area of the city that one never suspected existed. A slightly different direction of attention is all one needs to overlook something that is happening right before our eyes, like a robbery or a kidnapping.

The limitations that matter and sense perception impose on us affect every level of human awareness and cognition. But knowledge is also limited on the part of the object; for it is matter that is the principle of indeterminacy, and so it is matter that renders substances opaque to the intellect. [20] It does this in two ways: both intrinsically and by virtue of the sheer multiplicity that matter permits.

Indeterminacy is not a principle of intelligibility, but the opposite, and that principle is an intrinsic principle of material substance. For example, the wood (which is not ultimate matter) that the carpenter uses to make something is indeterminate in relation to the artifact he intends to make (indeed, wood is not pure indeterminacy, but a determinate substance, namely wood). Without that artificial form (i.e., desk, or shelving unit, or cupboards, etc.), we don't know what that wood is going to become. But when the product is made, the wood remains the principle of indeterminacy or potentiality, rendering the artifact mutable, that is, able to be reshaped into something else. By analogy, the ultimate principle of potentiality (the indeterminacy of prime matter) is one of the first principles of material substance; the other is the principle of actuality, or substantial form. The substance is essentially intelligible by virtue of its substantial form, but it is this enduring principle of fundamental indeterminacy (prime matter) which is the subject of the form that renders the substance opaque to the understanding; for when the intellect abstracts the intelligible pattern or determination of a thing, its "whatness", that abstraction includes matter, that is, it includes the principle of indeterminacy or potentiality—what is this thing that I know? It is a material kind of thing, a mutable entity. Thus, what exists in my mind is not the formal principle alone, but the formal and material principle together, abstracted from the material conditions outside the mind (the thing does not exist in my mind physically, but logically). The potency/act unity exists in my mind and at the same time it exists outside my mind—it is existentially neutral.

A material thing is potentially intelligible, not actually intelligible. It is actually determined, but its essential intelligibility in all its universality must be abstracted out by the active mind. But that abstraction is not complete; knowing what a thing is depends on the activity of the thing, which unveils it, and we don't see things act all at once, but only partially, that is, gradually. Hence, we come to know "what" things are only in time.

Thus, coming to know what things are, their natures, is time consuming and depends on observing the activities of things from various angles and in the light of specific questions. Activity unveils a thing because the thing is material and extended into parts outside of parts. The indeterminacy of matter and quantity veils material things, so to speak. A material and quantified thing is actually something, something determinate, but it is not identical to its activity (activity is a secondary mode of being); its essential intelligible determination is wrapped up with the indeterminacy of matter. As a whole, a material thing exists in a state of potential unfolding. Everything it is, its meaning, is not immediately unraveled—nor can it ever be completely unraveled—, for the mind to apprehend its meaning requires that it move. It exists in time, thus it can move, and when it moves, it discloses, that is, what it is becomes gradually manifest.

But matter also limits the intelligibility of things collectively, by virtue of the sheer multiplicity that matter makes possible; for matter is one of the principles of individuation. For example, there is only one "humanness", but many humans, one "canine", but many dogs, etc. The form or essential determination of matter is one, but it is "signate" matter (matter considered under determinate dimensions)[21] that allows a form to be indefinitely multiplied in individual instances. Now oneness or unity is a property of being, so I am a single being by virtue of my unique act of existing; I am a single kind of being, that is, a human kind of being, an ordered entity, by virtue of the essential determination that is the substantial form (which is always in composition with prime matter, which makes mutability part of my essential determination); but I am not distinguished from my colleagues on the basis of my nature—for we all have the same nature. I am a unique and single being by virtue of my act of existing, which is diverse,[22] and I am a different material entity from another—who has the same nature—by virtue of my own signate matter. It is this material principle, not a formal principle, which allows a material kind of thing to be multiplied indefinitely, sort of like cookie dough that allows a figure (i.e., a cookie cutter) to be repeated indefinitely, to produce however many cookies we would like.

Multiplicity, as was said earlier, is a principle of indeterminacy, for it is unity that determines a plurality, thus rendering it intelligible in some way. But it is dimensive quantity that allows material substances to be multiplied into a number of instances, all having the same nature, and it is the sheer multiplicity of things that makes knowledge so difficult to achieve and statistical reasoning so necessary. There is not much that is opaque about a triangle divested of matter, but a triangle that exists in matter is something very different; it is subject to change and there are countless instances. Similarly, there is much less opacity to "rational animal", which defines man, than there is to questions about man that proceed from the effect to the cause. What this population thinks of the current leader or the latest fad diet is not something that can be deduced from a universal principle, only inferred on the basis of evidence gathered through random sampling and careful statistical reasoning that still leaves a space of uncertainty when all is said and done. And of course, the probability of the evidence given the hypothesis is not the same as the probability of the hypothesis given the evidence; confusing the two has been rather easy over the years.[23] Determining reasonable probability for conclusions not contained in the premises requires much more work, and the results are still, very often, surrounded by clouds of opacity, unlike abstract questions whose answers can be deduced from an understanding of their universal properties.

There are all sorts of epistemic conditions that make certain discoveries possible today that were not possible yesterday, and so our intellectual apprehension of reality, our interpretation of the total state of affairs of things, is always incomplete and in development, and dependent upon the insights of others.

Although knowledge at the higher levels of abstraction affords one greater certainty—these sciences are predominantly deductive—, it does so at the expense of detail (i.e., biology is richer than mathematics, for a plant or animal is richer in content than a number).[24] This relatively certain knowledge, nevertheless, is still limited by the limitations of the knower. In other words, it shares in the limitations that sense perception imposes on human knowing. The comparisons and analogies employed to illustrate a metaphysical idea may be false, or true from one angle and false from another; or one may overemphasize an idea which disposes him to overlook another idea, one that, if had, would open up a new avenue of inquiry that would permit the resolution of a host of unresolved questions, thereby spawning a host of new questions. Hence, not only is precise scientific knowledge relatively tentative, a vast portion of metaphysical insights are relatively tentative as well.

However, the different levels on which the philosophy of being and the experimental sciences operate are discontinuous. This is important to note, because sometimes philosophers will pronounce on matters of science (i.e., physics, or economics, or chemistry, etc.) from a higher level of abstraction. For example, it is not possible to pronounce on whether or not cutting taxes or lowering the minimum wage is prudent on the basis of general moral principles; one has to possess science, specifically the science of economics, in order to determine whether or not such decisions will raise a state's overall standard of living, that is, whether they are prudent in the here and now, and unfortunately determining such a thing requires far more labor than does abstract moral reasoning. Such crossing of boundaries would constitute an abuse of philosophy.

Conversely, sometimes scientists will try to derive philosophical conclusions on the basis of scientific premises, and this constitutes an abuse of science. It is not possible to pronounce on the ultimate nature of things, much less what it means 'to be', on the basis of knowledge acquired on the first level of abstraction. Consider the following dictum: "We see the world, not as it is, but as we are—or, as we are conditioned to see it" (Stephen Covey). When such a dictum is interpreted as a metaphysical statement—that being is not given in knowledge—, it is impossible for the statement to be true; for it would be impossible to know that we do not see the world as it is, but as we are, unless we can see the world as it is and compare that to how we previously saw it. On a more concrete level, however, the statement is indeed true. As Aristotle said, "...as a person is, so does the end appear to him". Moreover, an awareness of the cognitive biases that distort intuitive statistical reasoning and investigative activity corroborate the dictum. Coming to appreciate this, however, presupposes one is able to see the world as it is, for only then can we come to know the specific epistemic conditions that skew our perception of it.

But what if it is the other way around, namely, that it is not being that is given in knowledge, but it is we, the observer, who gives being (actuality or determination) to reality? Some popular scientists argue that although we can never measure the electron with perfect accuracy, we can determine what we will observe—a wave (if we refine our motion measurement) or a particle (if we refine our position measurement). What we observe depends on how we observe it. The observed phenomenon depends on the observation, and therefore on the observer. Hence, quantum theory raises serious doubts about the common sense belief in an objective world that is independent of our observations, or so some believe. Quantum theory and the uncertainty principle has established the point that we cannot picture nature but can only predict the results of specific experiments—and these results will depend on how we choose to perform our experiments. Thus, not only are we blind to the workings of nature, but even our brief glimpses are not of an objective, independent reality but of a subjective, observer-determined world.

Philosophy has no issue with quantum theory as such; but the interpretation of what that theory means ultimately in terms of knowledge and existence is not the domain of science, but philosophy. The following is a brief outline of a possible reply to such an interpretation.

Experiment is a special form of experience, a controlled experience. Now experience in general is prior to experiment; the latter is less general. And so if experience is purely subjective, that is, observer determined, then experiment and its results are purely subjective (unreliable from a realist point of view). In other words, what is happening here is that one begins with an experiment (a controlled experience) and through that experiment establishes a proposition (which will become a premise in an argument), namely, that we cannot be certain of the position and momentum of an electron at the same time; our determination of one is had at the expense of the other. That proposition is taken as an accurate description of a real and objective state of affairs. Taking this further into philosophical territory, a conclusion is ultimately reached that we do not see the world as it is in itself, that is, objectively; rather, the observer determines what he observes.

But that means that our first premise cannot be taken seriously, because it was established on the basis of an experiment, which is a controlled experience, and experience is un-objective or observer determined. Therefore, we cannot conclude that realism is false—we have no reliable premises from which to draw that conclusion. In fact, we cannot conclude anything about the relationship between the observer and the external world; much less can we conclude anything about the relationship between the observer and the electron. How can one start out as a realist in order to establish a premise, and then proceed to reason on the basis of that premise to deny realism? If one ends by denying realism, one must also deny the first premise of the argument that is derived from a realist standpoint, and if I deny the first premise, I cannot achieve my end, that is, I cannot conclude that realism is naive. It seems to me that quantum idealism is really an example of sawing off the branch on which one sits in order to observe the world.

16 Some Final Thoughts on Being and the Beautiful

Many times throughout this book we have said that whatever is, is one; if it is not one, it is many (beings). In other words, oneness or unity is a property of being. But what makes something beautiful is precisely unity. We live in a universe of quantified substances, and there is tremendous variety in this universe, i.e., a variety of things, colors, sounds, thoughts, words, possible heroic actions, etc. Now multiplicity is real, but multiplicity is unintelligible considered in itself, for multiplicity (or plurality) is a potentiality towards unity. It is intelligible only to the degree that it possesses unity. A plurality of nickels is intelligible insofar as we are talking about a unit of currency (5 cents, or a nickel); without further specification, we cannot determine just how many nickels we are talking about and thus how much money in total we are talking about. To the degree that we are left without unity, we are left with indeterminacy, and pure plurality is a pure lack of unity, or pure indeterminacy, which is completely unintelligible.

A beautiful work of art or a beautiful scene or a beautiful face, etc., all possess certain properties. Fundamentally, there is a unity to something that is beautiful and thus a certain intelligibility. What is completely unintelligible cannot be experienced as beautiful; if it is experienced as beautiful, even by only one person, it is experienced as having some degree of intelligibility. And if it has some degree of intelligibility, it possesses some kind of order; in other words, it possesses a kind of harmony or proportion. A lack of harmony or proportion is a lack of order, which boils down to a lack of determination. A multiplicity that is unified proportionately or harmoniously is more radiant to the intellect, that is, it is more intelligible; thus, it is more pleasing, because the intellect delights in intelligibility. It is pleased with determination.

To say this is not to say anything about the quality of a particular work of art, such as a Picasso, which might at first glance appear to lack proportion—what lacks proportion on one level might possess it on another; in fact, the lack of proportion on one level might be a condition for appreciating the proportion on a different level. Rather, we are speaking more generally, not specifically about any particular style of art.

Furthermore, what is beautiful will also be experienced as complete or integral. What is incomplete is unfinished and to that degree unsatisfying, for it is insufficient. Whatever is incomplete tends to a terminal, but fails to reach it. To this degree, the work is displeasing to the intellect.

Beauty, it would seem, is a property of being, for the properties of beauty are unity, intelligibility, and proportion, which are all properties of being. In other words, unity, intelligibility and proportion are together necessary and sufficient conditions for the beautiful. Whatever is, is one, intelligible, and proportioned, and whatever is proportioned, intelligible and one is experienced as beautiful.

Parmenides, the first metaphysician, concluded that being is spherical. It is difficult to know what he meant by this. Perhaps he meant that being is symmetrical, for what is symmetrical is one, simple, ordered, and radiant with intelligibility. Being as such is not spherical, at least not literally, because being is indivisible--which Parmenides understood—, and a sphere is divisible. But a sphere is symmetrical: all points on the surface are the same distance from the center; moreover, there is a certain efficiency to a sphere in that it has the smallest surface area for a volume. A sphere is a thing of beauty; for the greater the unity, the greater the symmetry. Whether mathematical, or philosophical, or scientific, an idea within a particular area of study that possesses greater scope is experienced as more satisfying, for it has greater intellectual sufficiency, because it explains more, covers more ground, like the exhilarating view from a mountain top. An idea that covers more with less work is more efficient, and the greater the scope, the greater the exhilaration. Perhaps this is why physicists search for the formula for a theory of everything. If such a mathematical formula is eventually discovered, I believe it is a safe guess that it will be a formula of tremendous simplicity, beauty, and depth.

There is no doubt that coming to an agreement about what constitutes a thing of beauty, such as a beautiful work of art, is often impossible, but it seems to me indisputable that certain conditions are required in order to be able to appreciate a truly beautiful work of art. In other words, beauty is really in the work, not merely in the one who beholds the work, but the subject beholding the work must be disposed in a particular way, that is, he requires certain epistemic conditions without which he will not behold the beauty in the work. Anyone who has developed any kind of artistic skill knows this from within; initially, the beginner thinks his work is quite good; after advancing to a higher level, he suddenly realizes how bad his earlier work really is, whether we are talking about singing, playing an instrument, painting, sculpture, or writing, etc. For some skills, competency is a necessary condition for recognizing incompetence, one's own included, which would explain why those of lesser competence—in some areas at least—overestimate their competence, while the competent typically underestimate their competence.[25]

From these principles, I believe it follows quite readily that God, who is being itself, is supremely and unlimitedly beautiful and the source of all beauty. In the physical universe, it is the intellect that is the simplest power, for it grasps the simplest idea, namely being. The higher up we proceed on the scale of the hierarchy of being of material substances, the simpler beings become, at least from one angle. Indeed, a carbon atom is simpler than a horse, but a horse has everything the carbon atom has and more. The horse can become, cognitively, the object it perceives without ceasing to be what it is and without changing the object of its perception. The horse can take in the valley in a single glance—it exists in him (in his senses, to a limited extent, of course). The human person, on the other hand, becomes whatever he knows in an immaterial way, and so his becoming 'other' is far more extensive (i.e., he possesses universal ideas and can arrive at certain conclusions not empirically verifiable). Angels, however, are simpler still, for they are intelligences pure and simple, without the complexities of matter and sense perception, while God is wholly without composition; for whatever exists in God is identical to his act of existing. In other words, God is beauty itself.

In this light, all science and every quest for knowledge is, ultimately, a search for God. The awe inspiring beauty of the universe is a seemingly inexhaustible work of prose announcing its origin; the mathematical infinity of the universe is a verse that announces the infinity of its origin, and the physical finitude of the universe is a different verse declaring that nothing compares to God, the beginning and end of all things who is truly without limits. If this God—the origin and end of all things who exists necessarily, whom we can know about only indirectly and very abstractly—were to reveal himself directly in a way proportioned to our natural mode of knowing, the content of that revelation would be much richer than anything that can be deductively inferred by the natural light of reason—just as history is much richer than metaphysics. To know it and adhere to it would require faith, since its content would exceed reason's ability to apprehend. Indeed, most of what we hold to be true is only a matter of natural faith in the sense of trusting what someone tells you, because you have evidence that the speaker is informed and trustworthy. Such a natural faith is necessary, for we could not function without it, for human beings are far too limited. In this sense, natural faith is entirely reasonable. Faith in the content of divine revelation, however, would have to be of an entirely different nature, because its content would transcend reason. It would have to be a faith that is supra-natural because it is supra-rational. Such a faith would not necessarily be unreasonable—unless of course it contradicted reason—, but neither would it be demanded by reason, unlike natural faith. It would, however, exceed our natural capacity, so it would have to be created in us. If such a virtue is possible, it can only be received as a sheer gift.

About the Author

Douglas McManaman studied Philosophy at St. Jerome's College in Waterloo, and Theology at the University of Montreal. He was a regular columnist for the Canadian Messenger of the Sacred Heart and Catholic Insight Magazine, and continues to write for Lifeissues.net, and the Catholic Educator's Resource Center. He is the author of *Why Be Afraid?* (Justin Press), *The Logic of Anger* (Justin Press), *Basic Catholicism, Introduction to Philosophy for Young People, A Treatise on the Four Cardinal Virtues,* and *Readings in the Theory of Knowledge: A Primer for Young People.* He has been interviewed four times on EWTN Radio, The Good Fight with Barbara McGuigan. He is a Permanent Deacon for the Archdiocese of Toronto and the current chaplain of the Catholic Teachers Guild. He has been teaching Religion and Philosophy to senior high school students for 30 years; he is currently teaching at Father Michael McGivney Catholic Academy in Markham, Ontario, Canada. He is the past president of the Canadian Fellowship of Catholic Scholars.

Endnotes

---

¹ Science and scientism are not the same thing. Science in general is a knowledge of things through their proper causes; scientism is the philosophical school of thought that maintains that the only valid knowledge is that which is acquired through the empiriometric sciences (i.e., physics, chemistry, biology, etc.).

² "Thus God alone (or the necessary Being) has this prerogative that He must necessarily exist, if He is possible. And as nothing can interfere with the possibility of that which involves no limits, no negation and consequently no contradiction, this [His possibility] is sufficient of itself to make known the existence of God *a priori*. We have thus proved it, through the reality of eternal truths. But a little while ago we proved it also *a posteriori*, since there exist contingent beings, which can have their final or sufficient reason only in the necessary Being, which has the reason of its existence in itself." Gottfried Wilhelm Leibniz. *The Monadology*, 45; trans. Robert Latta. GP 4, 406.

³ The antecedent is the "if" clause of a hypothetical syllogism, the consequent is the "then" clause. For example, "If you contract some form of food poisoning, then you will be sick". An unknown antecedent is a hypothesis, the consequent is the evidence available.

⁴ Jacques Maritain. *A Preface to Metaphysics*, London, Sheed and Ward, 1948. Pp. 97-105.

⁵ Nietzsche is very useful here, for he is one of the most consistent thinkers in the history of philosophy, at least as consistent as one can possibly be when one denies being in favor of pure becoming; the result is that reality is absurd and thus unknowable. All science becomes a fiction:

"Not "to know" but to schematize—to impose upon chaos as much regularity and form as our practical needs require.

In the formation of reason, logic, the categories, it was *need* that was authoritative: the need, not to "know," but to subsume, to schematize, for the purpose of intelligibility and calculation—(The development of reason is adjustment, invention, with the aim of making similar, equal—the same process that every sense impression goes through!) No pre-existing "idea" was here at work, but the utilitarian fact that only when we see things coarsely and made equal do they become calculable and usable to us— Finality in reason is an effect, not a cause: life miscarries with any other kinds of reason, to which there is a continual impulse—it becomes difficult to survey—too unequal—... The subjective compulsion not to contradict here is a biological compulsion: the instinct for the utility of inferring as we do infer is part of us, we almost *are* this instinct— But what naiveté to extract from this a proof that we are therewith in possession of a "truth in itself"!— Not being able to contradict is proof of an incapacity, not of "truth."

...If, according to Aristotle, the law of contradiction is the most certain of all principles, if it is the ultimate and most basic, upon which every demonstrative proof rests, if the principle of every axiom lies in it; then one should consider all the more rigorously what *presuppositions* already lie at the bottom of it. Either it asserts something about actuality, about being, as if one already knew this from another source; that is, as if opposite attributes *could* not be ascribed to it. Or the proposition means: opposite attributes *should* not be ascribed to it. In that case, logic would be an imperative, not to know the true, but to posit and arrange a world that shall be called true by us. ...The "thing"— that is the real substratum of "A"; *our belief in things* is the precondition of our belief in logic. The "A" of logic is, like the atom, a reconstruction of the thing— If we do not grasp this, but make of logic a criterion of true being, we are on the way to positing as realities all those hypostases: substance, attribute, object, subject, action, etc.; that is, to conceiving a metaphysical world, that is, a "real world" (--this, however, is the apparent world once more--)." *The Will to Power,* translated by Walter Kaufmann and R. J. Hollingdale. New York: Vintage, 1968. Sections 515 and 516.

[6] Perfection, from the Latin *per factum*: 'made through'. To make something is to move a subject from potentiality to actuality. The manufacturing process ends when the form is realized in the matter. Hence, a perfection is an act, the realization of a potentiality.

[7] It is important to note that we are talking about a series of essentially subordinate movers, like the links in the chain holding up a chandelier, or a series of boxcars of a very long freight train.

[8] "To know that God exists in a general and confused way is implanted in us by nature, inasmuch as God is man's beatitude. For man naturally desires happiness, and what is naturally desired by man must be naturally known to him. This, however, is not to know absolutely that God exists; just as to know that someone is approaching is not the same as to know that Peter is approaching, even though it is Peter who is approaching; for many there are who imagine that man's perfect good which is happiness, consists in riches, and others in pleasures, and others in something else." *S.T.* I, q. 2, art 1, ad. 1.

[9] Rudy Rucker. *The Fourth Dimension: A Guided Tour of the Higher Universes* (Boston: Houghton Mifflin, 1984) 145-146.

[10] In the change from A to B, there must be something in B that was in A, otherwise A simply went out of existence, and B came into existence, which is to say that A did not change into B.

---

[11] What does it mean to be fundamentally the same artifact? Not every part is a fundamental part; perhaps the chassis of a car has endured, and so one can say it is fundamentally the same car, just as the foundation of a building is fundamental.

[12] Physicist Stephen Barr writes: "Modern physics has reached the same conclusion by a parallel route. Whereas St. Augustine started with the insight that time is something created, modern physics starts with the insight that time is something physical. After Einstein's theory of General Relativity, it became clear that space and time, rather than being something over and above physical events and processes, actually form a physical "space-time manifold" or fabric that is acted upon by other physical entities and acts upon them in turn. Space-time can bend and flex and ripple; and these distortions of space-time carry energy and momentum, just as all physical things do. Indeed, space-time is just as physical as magnetic fields are, or as rocks and trees." "Modern Physics, the Beginning, and Creation". Dec, 2013. PDF file. <http://washtheocon.org/wp-content/uploads/2013/12/Modern-Physics.pdf>.

[13] Perhaps it can be said that what is being advocated here is conceptual idealism. Subject and object are correlative terms; there is no objectivity without subjectivity. When a person writes a letter, his purpose is to communicate what is on his mind. Without an intelligent subject to receive the communication, the letter is perhaps nothing more than lines of ink and cellulose fibers. But of course, the letter is much more than that. Without an intelligent subject to receive the letter, the fullness of what it is objectively cannot be properly apprehended. Similarly, consider the claim that color and sound are not real, since without the perceiving subject, there are only sound waves and reflected light; and because sound waves are not sound and reflected light is not color, color and sound, so it is argued, are not objective qualities of things, that is, outside the mind and in the thing, but merely

within the perceiver. It seems to me that this reasoning involves the assumption that objectivity requires the elimination of subjectivity. The position I am taking here is that subjectivity is required in order to possess the objective, and so only through a subject who has the power to perceive is it possible to objectively grasp certain aspects of real existing beings, such as their colors and their sounds, just as it is only through an intelligent subject that the complete reality of that hunk of cellulose fibers with ink markings can be known. The reason for this is that being exists ultimately for a knower, that is, for intelligence. Nicholas Rescher points out: "The pivotal thesis of conceptual idealism is accordingly that we standardly think of reality in implicitly mentalesque terms. And this contention rests on two basic theses: 1. That *our* world, the world as we know it, is— inevitably—the world *as we conceive it to be,* and 2. That the pivotal concepts (thought-instrumentalities) that we standardly use in characterizing and describing this world contain in their make-up, somewhere along the line, a reference to the operations of mind. Observing that our "standard conception" of the world we live in is that of a multitude of particulars endowed with empirical properties and positioned in space and time and interacting causally, conceptual idealism goes on to maintain that all of the salient conceptions operative here—particularly, spatiotemporality, causality, and the possession of empirical (experimentally accessible) properties—are mind-involving..." *Philosophical Inquiries – An Introduction to Problems of Philosophy.* Pittsburgh, Pa: University of Pittsburgh Press, 2010. Chapter 4: "Realism/Idealism". [Kobo version]. Retrieved from http://www.kobo.com.

14 When we consider the thing in itself, it is a potency/act unity. What determines a material thing to be the kind (genos) of thing it is, is the substantial form, whose subject is first matter, which is pure potentiality. But when we consider

the thing in relation to the act of existing, the essence includes matter. The act of existing is the intelligibility of intelligibilities, because it is the act of all acts. Simple apprehension is the apprehension of the essential intelligibility of the being; existential judgment is the apprehension of the existential intelligibility of the being, or the apprehension of existence. The two acts of the intellect are simultaneous: if I apprehend that something is, I apprehend a "what" that exists; and of course I can only grasp a "what" by virtue of the fact that it exists. The definition of something expresses the essential intelligibility of a being, the intelligible limits that mark off where this being begins and ends, that is, what it is and what it is not. This limited and limiting nature really exists by virtue of the act of existing.

[15] Nicholas Rescher writes: "There is no practicable way in which the claim that science has achieved temporal finality can be validated. We can never legitimate an affirmative answer to the question, "Is the current state of science, S, final?" For the prospect of future changes of S can never be precluded. One cannot plausibly move beyond, "We have (in S) no good reason to think that S will ever change," to obtain, "We have (in S) good reason to think that S will never change." To take this posture toward S is to presuppose its completeness. It is not simply to take the natural and relatively unproblematic stance that that for which S vouches is to be taken as true but to go beyond this to insist that whatever is true finds a rationalization within S. This argument accordingly embeds finality in completeness, and in doing so jumps from the frying pan into the fire. For it shifts from what is difficult to what is yet more so. To hold that if something is so at all, then S affords a good reason to take so blatantly ambitious (even megalomaniacal) a view of S that the issue of finality seems almost a harmless appendage." *Ignorance: On the Wider Implications of Deficient*

Knowledge. Pittsburgh, Pa: University of Pittsburgh Press, 2009. Chapter 5: "On Limits to Science". [Kobo version]. Retrieved from http://www.kobo.com.

[16] Nicholas of Cusa writes: "Hence, the intellect, which is not truth, never comprehends truth so precisely that truth cannot be comprehended infinitely more precisely. For the intellect is to truth as [an inscribed] polygon is to [the inscribing] circle. The more angles the inscribed polygon has the more similar it is to the circle. However, even if the number of its angles is increased *ad infinitum*, the polygon never becomes equal [to the circle] unless it is resolved into an identity with the circle. Hence, regarding truth, it is evident that we do not know anything other than the following: viz., that we know truth not to be precisely comprehensible as it is. For truth may be likened unto the most absolute necessity (which cannot be either something more or something less than it is), and our intellect may be likened unto possibility. Therefore, the quiddity of things, which is the truth of beings, is unattainable in its purity; though it is sought by all philosophers, it is found by no one as it is. And the more deeply we are instructed in this ignorance, the closer we approach to truth. *On Learned Ignorance*. Bk I, ch. 3, sec 10. The translation of Book I was made from *De docta ignorantia. Die belehrte Unwissenheit*, Book I (Hamburg: Felix Meiner, 1970, 2nd edition), text edited by Paul Wilpert, revised by Hans G. Senger. PDF version, Retrieved from: http://jasper-hopkins.info/DI-I-12-2000.pdf.

[17] "Though intentional action is characteristic of all knowledge, both animal and human, there is something about the contact with being which stamps the intellect as a spiritual, simple thing working far above the highest altitude which the senses attain. Being, it was seen, is a simple thing in the sense of standing undivided; once divided, the so-called parts would be nothing since there is only the non-

being beyond being. So when being, a simplicity, is known, the tool that has delivered it to man must also be a simple thing." Vincent E. Smith, *Idea Men of Today*. Milwaukee: Bruce Publishing Company, 1950. 392.

[18] *Ignorance: On the Wider Implications of Deficient Knowledge*. Pittsburgh, Pa: University of Pittsburgh Press, 2009. Chapter 4: "Cognitive Finitude". [Kobo version]. Retrieved from http://www.kobo.com.

[19] Although mathematics is abstract and fairly universal (it abstracts from social context, from culture, and from the realm of the sensible), the development of the science of mathematics arises out of very specific problems; for example, the science of geometry began in Egypt out of a need to re-establish property boundaries after the flooding of the Nile, and astronomy arose out of Astrology and the problems it attempted to solve. It was the Greeks who studied the work of the Egyptians, but for its own sake, not for the sake of re-establishing property lines or for the sake of knowing what the future holds. Much of the history of science has its roots in specific problems to solve, whether economic, or military, etc.

[20] "There is, in principle, no end to the different lines of consideration available to yield descriptive truths, so that the totality of potentially available facts about a thing—about any real thing whatever—is bottomless. John Maynard Keynes's 'Principle of Limited Variety' is simply wrong: there is no inherent limit to the number of distinct descriptive kinds or categories to which the things of this world can belong. Who can ever say that there is not more to be said about something within nature's panoply of reals? As best we can possibly tell, natural reality has an infinite descriptive depth. It confronts us with a Law of Natural Complexity: There is in principle no limit to the number of natural kinds to which any concrete particular belongs. And this of course

means that reality has a cognitive profundity whose bottom we can never hope to fathom altogether. The world's things are cognitively opaque: we cannot see through to the bottom of them. And this is something about which, in principle, we cannot delude ourselves, since such delusion would vindicate rather than deny a reality of facts independent of ourselves. It is the very limitation of our knowledge of things". Nicholas Rescher. *Ignorance: On the Wider Implications of Deficient Knowledge.* Pittsburgh, Pa: University of Pittsburgh Press, 2009. Chapter 8: "Implications of Ignorance". [Kobo version]. Retrieved from http://www.kobo.com.

[21] See St. Thomas Aquinas. *On Being and Essence.* Ch. 2, 4-5.

[22] Dr. F. F. Centore writes: "Being is not a universally common nature of some especially shallow comprehension present in all that is and grasped by means of a single concept. Rather, the being of each individual essence is not only really diverse from that essence but diverse with respect to every other instance of essence and existence. This diversity can and must be apprehended separately in each and every case, and in each successive period of time, by means of judgment....Now, what would happen if the being of things was not diverse but only different? If such were the case, being would have to be viewed as some sort of *thing*, a super-genus, an especially denuded essence, underlying all that is. In fact, not just underlying in some prime matter sense but actually identified with all that is as a genus is identified with its species. Being would be *the* genus for everything? "A Note on Diversity and Difference". The Thomist, XXXVI, 3, July, 1972. P. 473.

[23] I am referring specifically to the fallacy of the transposed conditional. See Gerd Gigerenzer (2004). "Mindless statistics". The Journal of Socio-Economics 33. 587-606. DOI: 10.1016/j.socec.2004.09.033. 594-595.

[24] "There is in general an inverse relationship between the precision or definiteness of a judgment and its security: detail and reliability stand in a competing relationship." Nicholas Rescher, *Ignorance: On the Wider Implications of Deficient Knowledge*. Pittsburgh, Pa: University of Pittsburgh Press, 2009. Chapter 8: "Implications of Ignorance". [Kobo version]. Retrieved from http://www.kobo.com.

[25] "In essence, we argue that the skills that engender competence in a particular domain are often the very same skills necessary to evaluate competence in that domain— one's own or anyone else's. Because of this, incompetent individuals lack what cognitive psychologists variously term *metacognition* (Everson & Tobias, 1998), *metamemory* (Klin, Guizman, & Levine, 1997), *metacomprehension* (Maki, Jonas, & Kallod, 1994), or *self-monitoring* skills (Chi, Glaser, & Rees, 1982). These terms refer to the ability to know how well one is performing, when one is likely to be accurate in judgment, and when one is likely to be in error." Justin Kruger and David Dunning. "Unskilled and Unaware of It: How Difficulties in Recognizing One's Own Incompetence Lead to Inflated Self-Assessments." Journal of Personality and Social Psychology, 1999, Vol. 77, No. 6, 1121.

Suggested Reading

Anscombe, G.E.M, *Metaphysics and the Philosophy of Mind: The Collected Philosophical Papers of G. E. M. Anscombe, II*. Oxford: Basil Blackwell, 1981.

Centore, F. F, *Being and Becoming: A Critique of Post-Modernism*. New York: Greenwood, 1991.

———, *Theism or Atheism: The Eternal Debate*. Burlington, VT.: Ashgate, 2004.

Gilson, Etienne, *Being and Some Philosophers*. Toronto, Pontifical Institute of Mediaeval Studies, 1952.

———, *The Elements of Christian Philosophy*. New York: The New American Library. 1960.

Grisez, Germain, *Beyond the New Theism: A Philosophy of Religion*. Notre Dame: University of Notre Dame Press, 1975.

Maritain, Jacques, *A Preface to Metaphysics*. London, Sheed and Ward, 1948

———, *The Range of Reason*. New York: Charles Scribner's Sons, 1952.

———, *Approaches to God*. New York: Macmillan, 1954.

———, *Existence and the Existent: An Essay on Christian Existentialism*. Translated by Lewis Galantiere and

Gerald B. Phelan. New York: Image Books, 1956.

Owens, Joseph, *St. Thomas Aquinas on the Existence of God: Collected Papers of Joseph Owens*. Edited by John R. Catan. Albany: State University of New York Press, 1980.

_____, *Human Destiny: Some Problems for Catholic Philosophy*. Washington, D.C.: The Catholic University of America Press, 1985.

_____, *An Interpretation of Existence*. Houston, TX, Center for Thomistic Studies, 1985.

_____, *An Elementary Christian Metaphysics*. Houston, TX, Center for Thomistic Studies, 1985.

Rescher, Nicholas, *Luck: The Brilliant Randomness of Everyday Life*. Pittsburgh, Pa: University of Pittsburgh Press, 1995.

_____, *Complexity: A Philosophical Overview*. New Brunswick, NJ: Transaction Publishers, 1998.

_____, *Ignorance: On the Wider Implications of Deficient Knowledge*. Pittsburgh, Pa: University of Pittsburgh Press, 2009.

Stein, Edith, *Knowledge and Faith*. Trans. Walter Redmond. Washington, D.C.: ICS Publications, 2000.

_____, *Finite and Eternal Being: An Attempt at an Ascent to the Meaning of Being*. Trans. Kurt F. Reinhardt. Washington, D.C.: ICS Publications, 2002.

_____, *Potency and Act: Studies Toward a Philosophy of Being*. Trans. Walter Redmond. Washington, D.C.: ICS Publications, 2009.

Van Inwagen, Peter, *Metaphysics*. Boulder, CO: Westview Press, 2015.

Wilhelmsen, Frederick, *Being and Knowing: Reflections of a Thomist*. New York: Preserving Christian Publications, 1995.